SEO FITNESS WORKBOOK:

The Seven Steps to Search Engine Optimization Success on Google

2017 EDITION

BY JASON MCDONALD, PH.D.

© 2017, JM INTERNET GROUP

https://www.jm-seo.org/

Tel. 800-298-4065

CONTENTS

0

INTRODUCTION

Welcome to the *SEO Fitness Workbook, 2017 edition*! Fully revised and updated for 2017, this workbook explains how to succeed at *Search Engine Optimization (SEO)* in **seven steps**. SEO, of course, is the art and science of **getting your company, product,** or **service** to show at the **top** of relevant Google or Bing searches, for **free**. With most customers turning first to Google, Bing, or other search engines, SEO is your free gateway to more inquiries, more customers, and more sales.

SEO =

FREE ADVERTISING ON GOOGLE

Free advertising on Google? Yippie! On Bing? Double Yippie! But, here's the rub: **SEO seems really complicated**. Is it "too good to be true?"

Believe me, I understand your frustration with SEO and with the frauds, scoundrels, and dishonest robbers who plague my beloved SEO industry. I know the complaints, and I hear them often in my classes in the San Francisco Bay Area, including my very popular "Marketing without Money" class at Stanford Continuing Studies. Here are some of the most **common complaints**:

- We need to get our company to the top of Google for relevant keywords; our competitors are there, but we're not!
- Our website stinks. It not only looks terrible, but we don't even show for our own company name!
- We hired an SEO company, spent several thousands of dollars, and achieved nothing. So-called "SEO experts" are just thieves!

- I don't understand computers, can't write HTML, and I can't do SEO. Help!
- I pay attention to Google, and SEO seems to change constantly: there's no way we can keep up: Penguin, Panda, Semantic Search, and Mobile-Friendly Website Design. Doesn't Google constantly change the rules?
- We hired an obscure third world SEO firm, they built 50,000 blog links, and now we have been obliterated by Google's Penguin update.
- SEO is just too hard for anyone without a degree in Computer Science from Yale University to be able to do. We give up! (*They then start uncontrollably sobbing*).
- We'll just do AdWords (and spend thousands of dollars). Google clearly needs more money from struggling small businesses just like ours, so they can invest in self-driving cars and gourmet meals for their pampered employees!

I hear and feel your pain. I am just a regular guy, and I have been confronted with what I call **techtimidation** probably as much as you have.

TECHTIMIDATION =

THE USE OF JARGON BY TECHIES TO INTIMIDATE MERE MORTALS

However, I firmly believe that a little education, a lot of hard work, and some common sense are all you really need to succeed in SEO. The computer nerds (and Googlers) would like us all to believe SEO is difficult – no impossible – without a computer science degree.

Poppycock. Hokum. Hooey. Malarkey, Rubbish, Baloney and even B.S.!

You can do SEO. You can succeed at it. It is easier than you think.

The purpose of this book is to, **first**, make you believe in yourself, **second**, empower you with the basic knowledge of how the SEO game is played, and **third**, help you make a detailed SEO plan for your business.

More on this later.

Let's return to SEO, *the art and science of getting your product, service or company to the top of the search engines.*

Google Algorithm Updates

Recent years have seen some terrifying Google search engine algorithm updates, such as *Penguin, Panda, Hummingbird,* and *Pigeon. (Google algorithm updates are named after terrifying animals in the zoo).* In a nutshell, *Penguin* has been an algorithm attack against "low quality" links, and *Panda* has been an algorithm attack against poor quality content. In addition, Google has recently penalized sites that are not "mobile friendly" and made major changes to local search results (*Pigeon*). The local "snack pack" box on local searches like "pizza" or "plumber," for example, has been reduced to three listings, or in some cases just two results, wreaking havoc on local small businesses that depend on Google for customer inquiries.

Google's other moves towards so-called "semantic search" have been moves to embed "artificial intelligence" into the Google search engine. Google, in short, has been busy changing the rules of the SEO game.

Google makes changes, and we have to adapt.

But here's the good news: the **basics** haven't really changed, and if you stick to the **basics** according to "white hat" SEO – you'll be fine.

Let me repeat that:

the basics have not changed in SEO.

This workbook will explain what not to do, and what to do, to succeed at SEO in this post-*Penguin*, post-*Panda* world. And, it will also educate you on the unchanged basic rules of SEO success.

(If you don't know what *Panda* and *Penguin* are... don't worry – I'll explain later).

Back to SEO.

What is SEO? SEO, of course, is the art and science of getting your company, product, or service to the top of Google's organic (free) results. If you're a seller of "industrial fans," it means when customers search Google or Bing for "industrial fans," they see your company's product at the top of the search results. If you're a local business like a pizza restaurant or a probate attorney, it means showing at the top of Google for searches such as "pizza delivery" or "probate lawyers in Houston."

Why is SEO so valuable? Simply put, SEO is valuable because nearly everyone turns first to Google to find products, services, or companies and because SEO costs nothing (other than knowledge, blood, sweat and tears). SEO, in short, is **free** advertising on Google! And there ain't nothing better than free, is there? (*Well, a few things, but please keep your mind on the subject at hand*).

How the Process Works

Let's step back and ponder how the marketing process works on Google. Customers turn to Google first to find new products and services, new companies and consultants. They tend to ignore ads, and they tend to read and click through on the organic listings that show on page one of Google, especially the top three positions. Looking at it from the perspective of a small business, Google is the beginning of a chain of very valuable marketing events.

Ranking on Google for *free* means you are getting *free* advertising,

free advertising means *free* clicks from Google,

free clicks from Google mean *free* web traffic, and

free web traffic means more sales inquiries and ultimately more sales.

SEO essentially turns "free advertising" into "paid sales," which if you think about it for a moment, is an incredible return on investment!

(*Note that for most of the book I will refer to Google rather than search engines in general, or Google, Bing, and Yahoo specifically. (By the way, Bing powers Yahoo's search results, meaning there are really just two search engines in the USA, Canada, and Western Europe: Google and Bing). The good news is that the SEO methods to rank on Google will generally work just as well for Bing and Yahoo*).

An SEO Checkup

Some questions for you:

1. Do your potential customers use Google or Bing to find companies, products or services like yours?
2. Taking a common search query relevant to your company (e.g., "industrial fans," or "best pizza Tulsa"), do you see your company on Page 1 of Google, positions 1, 2, or 3? High on the page, or low on the page? Do you see yourself in the "local" results which occur for "local" searches such as personal injury attorney, CPA, or sushi?
3. Taking a whole bunch of relevant keyword search queries (*the "universe" of search terms by which customers might search for your company, product or service*), do you generally show up on Page 1 of Google, positions 1-3? positions 1-10?, or not at all?

If you *generally* appear on Page 1 of Google, and especially in the top positions 1, 2, or 3, for *all* your relevant keywords, you can stop reading this book. You pass with an A+. If you generally do not appear, then keep reading. Or if you appear only on some search queries, but not others, or if you're not really sure what the search queries are, then you need help.

If you have no idea what search word "queries," "positions" on Google, or "high" vs. "low" on the page mean, don't worry. Don't feel stupid. You need help, and I am going to teach you.

Isn't SEO Hard?

Well, that's what Google would like you to think (*so spend money on AdWords...*) And that's what many in the SEO industry would like you to think (*so pay us big consulting fees, and don't ask any questions!*)

I don't agree. SEO isn't easy, but it isn't exactly hard either.

I've taught thousands of people in my online classes, in classes in the San Francisco Bay Area, and in corporate workshops, and I can confirm there is a lot of confusion about SEO. People think it's hard, or impossible, or mysterious, and that's simply not correct.

SEO is Easy

Like Getting Fit is Easy

SEO, you see, is a lot like **physical fitness**. Although everyone can conceivably run a marathon, for example, few people make the effort to learn how and even fewer take the disciplined steps necessary to train for and ultimately finish a marathon.

Does that make running a marathon easy?

No.

But does that make running a marathon hard?

Not really.

Like running a marathon, SEO is **conceptually** simple (*exercise a lot, train with discipline, don't give up*) but **practically** hard (*you have to work at it nearly every day*).

And, of course, the Olympic champions don't just work *hard*, they work *smart*.

That's the beginning of the **good news**. If you just learn how to work smarter (not harder), you'll find that SEO isn't really that hard. And it gets better.

For one thing, you probably aren't really aiming to run an SEO marathon. You're probably aiming just to "get in shape," meaning to get to the top of relevant keywords that narrowly fit your industry and/or your geographic area. Your more modest goal of helping your business to get free advertising on Google via SEO means only basic knowledge is required, and only modest effort.

Indeed, once a small business website is in decent SEO-friendly shape, my guess is about five hours a week on "Internet marketing" will suffice to keep you at the top of Google. Results vary, of course, as every situation is unique. But SEO is much, much easier than you'd think.

You're Smarter than Your Competitors

Even better, in most industries, you'll find that your competitors are not that smart! Most industries are not as competitive in SEO as you would think, and metaphorically speaking, you don't have to run faster than the bear; you just have to run faster than your buddy!

> *Let me rephrase that. You are not competing against Google! You are competing against your competitors, and they aren't that much smarter than you. In fact, I bet they might even be dumber!*

Indeed, I'd wager that 90% or more of your competitors are doing little to nothing in terms of SEO. If you just make a modest effort, and if that effort is channeled with the effective knowledge I will teach you in this book, I'll wager that there's a very strong possibility that you'll be on page one of Google, if not in the very top positions.

As Yoda from Star Wars says:

> *"Do. Or do not. There is no try."*

The Seven Steps to SEO Success

This workbook guides you through the **seven steps** to successful SEO. Along the way, we'll set goals, understand technical details, and have fun. Along the way, I will be your "fitness coach" to explain how it all works and to motivate you to keep trying.

You can do this!

Throughout this workbook, I will share with you other examples of businesses that understand SEO and succeed using the **seven steps**.

The **seven steps to SEO fitness** are built on a philosophy of empowerment. Can you understand SEO? *Yes you can!* Can you implement SEO? *Yes you can!* It takes some knowledge, it takes some effort, but yes you can do it.

Before we dive in, allow me to share just a few more points of background.

» MEET THE AUTHOR

Well, first of all, who am I and what makes me an expert? My name is Jason McDonald, and I have been active on the Internet since 1994 (having invented the Internet along with Al Gore). I have been teaching SEO, AdWords, and Social Media since 2009 - online, in San Francisco, at Stanford University Continuing Studies, at workshops, and in corporate trainings. Over 3000 people have taken my paid trainings; over 25,000 my free webinars, and over 7,000 subscribers to my YouTube channel. I love figuring out how things work, and I love teaching others! SEO is an endeavor that I understand, and I want to empower you to understand it as well.

Learn more about me at https://www.jasonmcdonald.org/, at my corporate website https://www.jm-seo.org/, or be brave and email me a question or comment to j.mcdonald@jm-seo.net.

Don't believe I'm good at SEO, Google "Jason McDonald" (*I'm usually in the top three*), Google "SEO Expert San Francisco" (*you'll see me there*), Google "AdWords Expert Witness" (*Yes, I do legal work – there's good money in it, and I have a daughter in college*), or Google "SEO Classes Chicago" (*You'll see the JM Internet Group," my training and consulting company*). Here's a screenshot of *Bay Area SEO Consultant*:

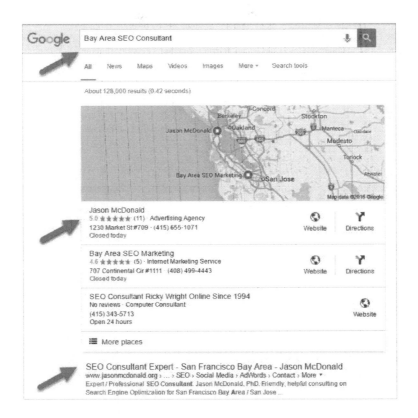

You can even Google "Best Books on SEO," and you'll usually see my booklist, with this book at the top of the list. Clever, huh?

Uncle? Give up? Still don't believe me? Call me up, or email me before you buy this book, and I'll give you reference examples of my SEO clients (*who don't want their competitors to know about me*).

≫ WHY THIS BOOK IS DIFFERENT

There are quite a few books on SEO out there! There are zillions of blog posts! There are thousands of SEO consultants! There are hundreds of crazy harebrained schemes...

But there is only one **workbook**: the *SEO Fitness Workbook*.

How is a *workbook* different from a *book*? Here's how.

First of all, this workbook speaks in **practical, no-nonsense English**. Whereas most of the SEO books out there are *by* experts *for* experts, this workbook explains SEO in plain English and does not get lost in the details. Most businesspeople don't need to know every gory detail about SEO; rather they need practical, hands-on advice about what to do first, second, third and so forth. The *SEO Fitness Workbook* is as much about "doing SEO" as it is about "understanding SEO."

Secondly, the *SEO Fitness Workbook* is **hands-on**. Most SEO books are meant to be passively read. *SEO Fitness Workbook*, by contrast, gives you "hands on" worksheets and deliverables. In fact, each chapter ends with a **DELIVERABLE** marked in **bold**. Each chapter also has **TODOS** (marked in **BOLD**) because a workbook is not just about reading, it's about **doing** and **succeeding**.

Third, while most books are outdated on the day they are published, the SEO Fitness Workbook connects to up-to-date **Internet resources** such as free SEO tools via the companion *SEO Toolbook*, and hands-on YouTube videos that show you how to succeed. After all, in the 21st century, a "how to" book should be more than a book, shouldn't it? It should be a gateway to up-to-date knowledge.

Fourth, within reason, I encourage you to reach out to me with your questions. Simply email j.mcdonald@jm-seo.net or visit https://www.jm-seo.org/contact. I truly enjoy the teaching of SEO, and I truly encourage my readers to ask questions. In fact, I learn as much from my students as they do from me because either I quickly know the answer to the question, or it's something weird and puzzling, and we'll learn the answer together. Don't be shy!

» REGISTER YOUR WORKBOOK FOR FREE ONLINE RESOURCES

Please **register** your *Workbook*. You'll not only get a full-color PDF copy of this *Workbook* to download with active, clickable links to the resources (very handy to read at your computer). You'll also get my updated *SEO Toolbook*, my secret *SEO Dashboard*, and all the Workbook's companion worksheets to help you step-by-step.

To register, follow these easy steps:

1. Go to the **JM Internet Group** Website, click on "Register Your Workbook," or just go directly to https://www.jm-seo.org/workbooks/
2. Click on "SEO Fitness Workbook 2017"
3. Enter your passcode: **2017fitness**.
4. If you have any problems, contact me via https://www.jm-seo.org/contact/ or call 800-298-4065 for help.

Sign up for email alerts at https://jm-seo.org/free, and - last but not least- watch a few of my YouTube videos at https://www.youtube.com/jmgrp; you'll find I am as crazy and enthusiastic on video as I am in this book!

New for 2017: Videos (More Videos)

I appreciate all the feedback from book readers in 2016, and the #1 item they asked for is more **videos**! Accordingly, I have beefed up my YouTube channel with even more videos, showing step-by-step various tips, tricks, and techniques for effective SEO. Check out the new videos at https://www.youtube.com/jmgrp or, as you read the book, I identify relevant videos topic-by-topic so you can pause, jump over to YouTube, watch a video and come back.

Access Jump Code Links

Note: throughout this book I use the website http://jmlinks.com/ to point to resources. You can either click on the resource directly in the book (if you're reading in digital format). Or, simply go to http://jmlinks.com/ and enter the **JUMP code**. For example, to visit http://jmlinks.com/7a simply go to http://jmlinks.com/ and enter "**7a**". That will take you to the referenced Internet resource.

> **VIDEO.** Watch a video tutorial of how to use the jump codes at http://jmlinks.com/jump or just visit http://jmlinks.com/ directly and enter *jump*.

» WHO THIS BOOK IS FOR

I have written *SEO Fitness Workbook* for the following groups of practical business folk:

Small Business Owners. If you own a small business that gets (or could get) significant customer traffic from the Web, this book is for you.

Small Business Marketers. If you are in charge of marketing for a small business that gets (or could get) significant customer traffic from the Web, this book is for you.

Marketing Managers. If you lead a Web team of inside or outside bloggers, SEO content writers, or other Internet marketing technicians including external SEO companies, this book is for you.

Web Designers. If you design websites but want to design sites that not only look good but actually rank high on Google search, this book is for you.

Non-profit Marketers. If you work at a non-profit or governmental agency that depends on Web search traffic, then this book is also for you.

Anyone whose organization (and its products, services, or other offerings) would benefit from being at the top of Google, for free, can benefit from the *SEO Fitness Workbook*.

» THE SEVEN STEPS TO SEO FITNESS: TABLE OF CONTENTS

Here are the seven steps to SEO fitness:

1. **Goals**: Define Your Goals
2. **Keywords**: Identify Keywords
3. **On Page SEO:** Get Your Website to "Speak Google"
4. **Content Marketing**: Create Quality Content for Google and for Humans
5. **Off Page SEO**: Build Links, Leverage Social Media, and Go Local
6. **Metrics**: Measure and Learn from Your Results
7. **Learn**: Never Stop Learning!

And here are the seven steps to SEO fitness in more detail –

Step #1: GOALS. SEO, like physical fitness, SEO is purpose-driven! You can't achieve your goals if you don't define what they are.

1.1 Attitude – attitude is everything, and SEO requires a commitment to learning how SEO works as well as a desire to implement positive SEO-friendly changes. Goal 1.1 is to have the right attitude. **PAGE: 22**

1.2 Goals – define what you sell, who your customers are, and how best to reach them. Define website goals such as to get online sales or acquire customer names, phone numbers, and email addresses as sales leads. **PAGE: 30**

1.3 Basics – understand the basics of SEO, i.e. "on page" and "off page" tactics. Goal 1.3 is to understand the SEO game at its most basic level. **PAGE: 40**

Step #2 KEYWORDS – identify your keywords. Keywords drive nearly every aspect of SEO, so you need a well-structured, clearly defined "keyword worksheet."

2.1 Keywords – identify high volume, high value keywords. **PAGE: 48**

2.2 Keyword Worksheet – build a keyword worksheet and measure your rank on Google and Bing. **PAGE: 70**

Step #3 ON PAGE SEO for your website. Once you know your keywords, where do you put them? It begins with page tags, proceeds through website organization, and ends with an "SEO audit" that outlines your SEO strategy. The nerd word for this is "on page" SEO.

3.1 Page Tags – understand basic HTML tags, and weave your target keywords into strategic tags such as the TITLE, META DESCRIPTION, and IMG ALT tags. **PAGE: 90**

3.2 Website Structure – build landing pages, restructure your home page, and optimize website layout through keyword-heavy link sculpting. **PAGE: 112**

3.3 SEO Audit – now that you know the basics of "on page" SEO, conduct an "on page" SEO audit of your website. **PAGE: 132**

Step #4 CONTENT MARKETING. They say that "content is king" in terms of SEO, and they are right. In this section, you'll create a long-term content strategy that moves beyond the "quick fix" of your site to a day-by-day, week-by-week system of SEO-friendly content.

4.1 Content SEO – devise a content strategy, specifically who will do what, when, where, how, and how often – that is, a short and long term SEO content marketing strategy including an inventory of the content you need to succeed. **PAGE: 138**

4.2 Press Release SEO - leverage news and free syndication services for SEO, because press releases are an easy technique to get links and build buzz on social media. **PAGE: 150**

4.3 Blogging – set up a blog that follows best SEO practices, including all-important connections to social media platforms like Google+ and Twitter. **PAGE: 160**

Step #5 OFF PAGE SEO – links and social media. "Off page" SEO leverages external web links and social media to boost your website's authority on Google. Use the traditional tactic of getting relevant inbound links. Then, leverage social media platforms like Twitter, Google+, Facebook, LinkedIn and YouTube to enhance your SEO efforts!

5.1 Link Building – conduct a link building audit and create a long-term link building strategy. **PAGE: 170**

5.2 Social Media SEO – look for social media mention opportunities, and enable relevant social profiles to enhance Google's trust in your website as an authoritative resource. **PAGE: 194**

5.3 Local SEO – local SEO stands at the juncture of SEO, local, and review based marketing, and so we dive into how to optimize a website for local searches. **PAGE: 206**

Step #6 METRICS – measure and learn from your results. Like physical fitness, SEO is a process that starts with a defined set of goals and employs specific measurements about goal achievement.

6.1 Metrics - measure your progress towards the top of Google, inbound keywords, and paths taken by customers once they land on your website. **PAGE: 226**

Step #7 LEARN - never stop learning. SEO starts with self-discovery, proceeds through technical knowledge, and ends with the hard work of implementation.

7.1 Learning – use Chapter 7 to get access to companion **worksheets** and the very important *SEO Toolbook* and my *secret dashboard*, which provide hundreds of free SEO tools, tools to help you in all aspects of SEO, from identifying keywords through page tags to links and social mentions. **PAGE: 241**

▶ SPREAD THE WORD: TAKE A SURVEY & GET $10 OR A FREE EBOOK!

If you like the book, please take a moment to provide honest feedback. Here's my special offer for those eager enough to take a short survey –

1. **Visit** http://jmlinks.com/survey.
2. **Compete** the survey on the book, as indicated.
3. Include your **email address** and **any feedback** (good, bad, positive, negative) about the book).
4. I will gift you $10.00 via Amazon gift eCard or send you one of my other books such as *AdWords Gotchas*, the *Social Media Workbook*, or my new *Job Search and Career-building Workbook*.

This offer is subject to change without notice. Offer expires 3/1/2017.

▶ QUESTIONS AND MORE INFORMATION

I **encourage** my students to ask questions. If you have questions, submit them via the **JM Internet Group Website** at http://jmlinks.com/contact by phone to 800-298-4065, or via email to j.mcdonald@jm-seo.net. There are two sorts of questions: ones that I know instantly, for which I'll zip you an email answer right away, and ones I do not know instantly, in which case I will investigate and we'll figure out the answer together.

As a teacher, I learn most from my students. So please don't be shy!

- *Jason McDonald, Ph.D.*

▶ COPYRIGHT AND DISCLAIMER

This is a completely **unofficial** guide to SEO. Neither Google nor Bing / Yahoo have <u>endorsed this guide</u>, nor has Google, Bing, or Yahoo nor anyone affiliated with Google, Bing, or Yahoo been involved in the production of this guide.

That's a *good thing*. This guide is **independent**. My aim is to "tell it as I see it," giving you no-nonsense information on how to succeed at SEO.

In addition, please note the following:

- All trademarks are the property of their respective owners. I have no relationship with nor endorsement from the mark holders. Any use of their marks is so I can provide information to you.

- Any reference to or citation of third party products or services whether for Google, Yahoo, Bing, or otherwise, should not be construed as an endorsement of those products or services tools, nor as a warranty as to their effectiveness or compliance with the terms of service of Google, Yahoo, or Bing.

The information used in this guide has been reviewed and updated as of December, 2016. However, SEO changes rapidly, so please be aware that scenarios, facts, and conclusions are subject to change without notice.

Additional Disclaimer. Internet marketing is an art, and not a science. Any changes to your Internet marketing strategy, including SEO, Social Media Marketing, and AdWords, is at your own risk. Neither Jason McDonald nor the JM Internet Group nor Excerpti Communications, Inc. assumes any responsibility for the effect of any changes you may, or may not, make to your website or AdWords advertising based on the information in this guide.

» ACKNOWLEDGEMENTS

No man is an island. I would like to thank my beloved wife, Noelle Decambra, for helping me hand-in-hand as the world's best moderator for our online classes, and as my personal cheerleader in the book industry. Gloria McNabb has done her usual tireless job as first assistant, including updating this edition as well the *SEO Toolbook*. My daughter, Ava, inspired me on YouTube, and my daughter, Hannah, has inspired me with her grit and determination to master subjects such as chemistry, biology, and physics as a Senior at Carnegie Mellon University. Last but not least, my black Lab

Buddy, kept my physically active and pondering the mysteries of Google on many jaunts through the San Francisco Bay Area.

And a huge thank you to my students – online, in San Francisco, and at Stanford Continuing Studies. You challenge me, you inspire me, and you motivate me!

1.1

ATTITUDE

Most books on SEO start with the technical details. What's a TITLE tag? How do you understand your Google PageRank? Which factors in the Google algorithm have changed recently? We'll get to all that, but I want to start this book with a pep talk about **attitude**.

Attitude, they say, is everything.

And nowhere is that more true than in SEO. This is an industry full of information overload, pretty rude intimidators of a technical geeky type, and an 800 lb Gorilla (Google), that would really rather you just spend money on AdWords advertising than understand how you can get to the top of Google without paying it a penny.

To succeed, you'll need a positive, "can do" attitude.

Let's get started!

TODO LIST:

>> Learn from Francie Baltazar-Schwartz that "Attitude is Everything."

>> Identify "Can Do" vs. "Can't Do" People.

>> Learn to Measure.

>> >> Deliverable: Inventory Your Team & Get Ready.

>> FRANCIE BALTAZAR-SCHWARTZ AND ATTITUDE IS EVERYTHING

The Internet is a wonderful place, and Google sits pretty much at the center of it. Got a question? "Just *Google* it!" We certainly know the reality of "Just *Google* it" in terms of customers look for companies, products and services. But it also goes for more important questions like the *meaning of life* (*42*), and *what is a LOL cat*, anyway?

For example, Google "Who said 'Attitude is Everything?'" and you'll find out that this quote is attributed to one Francie Baltazar-Schwartz. You can read it at http://jmlinks.com/5i. The point of "attitude is everything" is that you have two choices every day: either to have a **positive**, **can-do** attitude or to have a **negative**, **can't do** attitude. (**Remember**: if you are reading this book in print format, visit http://jmlinks.com/ and enter the JUMP code, in this case "**5i**").

This relates very dramatically to success at SEO, just as it does to success in pretty much everything else in life from physical fitness to your job to your marriage.

How does it apply to SEO? Well, let's look at the facts and let's look at the ecosystem of people and companies in the SEO industry.

Fact No. 1. SEO is technical, and at least on the surface, seems pretty complicated and hard. So, if you start out with the attitude that you "can't do it," you're already on the path to defeat. If, in contrast, you start with the attitude that you can do it, that other people are clearly doing it (*people no smarter than you*), you're on the path to success. **Attitude is everything.**

Fact No. 2. Google does not want anyone to believe that SEO is easy. In fact, because Google makes its money from *advertising* (nearly 90% of nearly $20 billion per quarter - see http://jmlinks.com/13k), it wants you, too, to believe that *advertising* is the way to go. Google has no incentive to explain how SEO works, and in fact, has every incentive to do the opposite. *If you are intimidated by Google, you're already on the path to defeat.* If, in contrast, you pay attention to the facts and realize that SEO is free, while ads cost money, that you can do SEO, and that you can get to the top of Google for free... you won't worry about the propaganda from a multibillion dollar corporation. **Attitude is everything.**

Fact No. 3. The SEO industry is full of so-called experts, gurus, tools providers and others who pretty much make their money by intimidating normal folk into believing that SEO is incredibly complicated and only nerds with Ph.D.'s in computer science can do it. They want you to stay in a state of dependency and keep paying them the big bucks... So if you allow technical nerds to intimidate you, you're already on the path to defeat. If, in contrast, you realize that they aren't really any smarter than you and that SEO isn't just about technology, it's about words and concepts and marketing messages, you're on the path to success. **Attitude is everything.**

Oh, and as SEO becomes more and more social, you'll want to have an open mind about social media as well. You can really get yourself motivated by watching a video by "Kid President" (Robby Novak), who is twelve years old, has 1.8 million views on YouTube, and was actually invited to the White House.

> **VIDEO.** Watch a "Can Do" attitude video by "Kid President" at http://jmlinks.com/5j.

For your first **TODO**, therefore, concentrate your mind and create a **positive attitude**: this is going to be fun, this is going to be educational, this is going to be a journey! Your **attitude is everything** as to whether you'll succeed or fail at SEO!

In fact, since the video screenshot was taken, this video now tops 39.4 million views as of December, 2016! If a *twelve-year-old* can get 39 million views and meet the President, don't you think you can at least get to page one of Google?

⏩ IDENTIFY "CAN DO" VS. "CAN'T DO" PEOPLE

In most situations, you'll need to depend on other people. Now the attitude of the people in your team (your webmaster, your content writers, your product marketing managers, your executives...) is also incredibly important. Are they "can do" or "can't do" sort of folks?

Henry Ford, the great industrialist, once made this clear observation:

> "Whether you think you can, or you think you can't--you're right."
> — Henry Ford

In terms of SEO, there are those people who think that a) they can't learn it, or b) it can't be done. And, guess what: they're **right**. And there are those who think that a) they can learn it, and b) it can be done. And, guess what: they're **right**, too.

Which camp are you in? Your team members? Can, or can't?

So for your second **TODO**, look around your organization and make a list of those people who need to be involved with your SEO project. For example:

Management and Marketers. These people are involved in the sense of understanding who your customers are, what you sell, and what the sales objectives are for your website. Your website, after all, isn't an end in itself but a means to an end: more sales.

Content Writers. Who writes (or will write) content for the website? These people need at least a basic understanding of your keywords and, even better, an understanding of how "on page" SEO works so that they know where to strategically place keywords on web content.

Web Designers. News flash: your website isn't just for humans! It's also for Google. You'll have to educate your web design team that your website needs to "talk" to Google just as much as it "talks" to humans. As we will learn, what Google likes (*text*) isn't generally what people like (*pictures*).

Web Programmers. The folks who program the backend, like your URL structure, your XML sitemaps and all that technical stuff. Who are these people and how will you get them on board for the SEO project?

Social Media and Outreach Experts. Social media is the new wave in SEO, so you'll need those folks who are (or will be) active on Twitter, Google+, YouTube, Facebook and the like to be "SEO aware," in the sense of how social media impacts SEO performance. You'll also need people to "reach out" to get inbound links to your website (more later).

Indeed, if you have some really obstructionist "Can't Do" people, you'll need to strategize either how to a) **persuade** them to participate, b) **get them out of the way**, or c) **work around** them.

≫ LEARN TO MEASURE

As you assemble your team, you'll want to get their buy in on learning SEO. It isn't a rocket science, but it's also not something you'll learn in a day. First, they'll need to learn the basics (See Chapter 1.3). Second, they'll need to learn many of the more esoteric topics as needed. Content writers, for example, will need to be keenly aware of keywords and how to write semantically friendly SEO text. Web programmers will need to understand XML sitemaps and so on. Third, they'll need to be committed to lifelong learning, as SEO changes over time. A good strategy is to schedule monthly meetings or corporate email exchanges about your SEO progress.

Let's also talk a little about **measurement** and **metrics**. One of the biggest stumbling blocks to successful SEO is the idea that it can't be measured. It can. How so?

Know your keywords. Once you know your keywords, as you'll learn in Chapter 2.1, then you can start to measure your **rank** on target Google searches.

Inbound search traffic. Once you set up Google Analytics properly as you'll learn in Chapter 6.1, you can measure your inbound "organic" traffic from Google, including data on inbound keywords. You'll learn how people get to your website, and what they do once they get there.

Goals. Every good website should have defined goals, usually registrations and/or sales. Once you define goals in Google Analytics, you can track what traffic converts to a sale, and what doesn't. (Then you can brainstorm ways to improve it).

When you first start, you'll often have little idea of your target keywords, little idea of your rank on Google, and little idea of your traffic patterns from landings to conversions. But that doesn't mean SEO isn't a measurable activity! It just means you are not yet measuring.

Why is this important? As you set up your team, and establish the right attitude, you want to establish the idea that SEO is measurable. If someone has crazy ideas (like Google doesn't pay attention to URL structure, or keywords don't matter), you can measure these ideas vs. correct ideas (keywords in TITLE tags matter a great deal, keyword-heavy URL's help a lot). Establishing a culture of measurability will help you get everyone on your team, even the most recalcitrant "Can't Do" people to realize that SEO works, and SEO can get your website to actually generate sales or sales leads.

Measurability is a critical part of Step No. 1: **Setting (Measurable) Goals**.

»» DELIVERABLE: INVENTORY YOUR TEAM AND GET READY

Now we've come to the end of Step 1.1, your first **DELIVERABLE** has arrived. Open up a Word document and create a list of all the people who are involved with your website, from the marketing folk who identify the goals (sales or registrations?), to the content writers (those who create product descriptions, blog posts, or press releases), to the Web design people (graphic designers), to the Web programmers, and to your outreach team for social media and links. Make an inventory of who needs to be involved in what aspects of SEO, and if possible, set up weekly or monthly meetings about your SEO strategy.

At a "top secret" level, you might also want to indicate who has a "Can Do" and who has a "Can't Do" attitude. You'll want to work to bring everyone over into the "Can Do" column!

Consider having an "attitude is everything" meeting about SEO, and get everyone to stand up on the tabletops and shout: "We can do this!"

SURVEY OFFER

CLAIM YOUR $10 REBATE OR FREE BOOK! HERE'S HOW –

1. Visit http://jmlinks.com/survey.
2. Take a short, simple survey about the book.
3. Indicate whether you want a $10.00 rebate or a free copy of one of Jason's other books on SEO / Social Media Marketing / Job Search & Career-building.

WE WILL THEN –

- Rebate you the $10.00, or send you a free copy of one of the other books.

~ $10 REBATE OFFER ~

~ LIMITED TO ONE PER CUSTOMER ~

EXPIRES: 3/1/2017

SUBJECT TO CHANGE WITHOUT NOTICE

GOT QUESTIONS? CALL 800-298-4065

1.2

GOALS

SEO, like physical fitness, can't be accomplished without **goals**. Are you training for a marathon, or a sprint? Want to look better at the beach, or just be healthier? Want to dominate Google for "industrial fans," for "organic baby food," or for "probate attorney St. Louis?" Is the purpose of your website to get sales leads, or to sell products via eCommerce? SEO can tell you *how* to get to the top of Google, but it can't tell you *what* your company's *goals* are vis-à-vis potential customers. To succeed at SEO, you need to have a clear vision of your *sales ladder* starting at the customer *need* and then proceeding as follows: keyword search *query* → *landing* on your website → sales *inquiry* → *back* and *forth* → actual *sale*. For an eCommerce site, the goals and sales ladder would be the same, except that rather than a "sales inquiry" the goal would be an actual website purchase.

Let's get started!

TODO LIST:

>> Define Your Business Value Proposition

>> Identify Your Target Customers by Segment

>> Establish Marketing Goals

>> >> Deliverable: A Business Value Proposition Worksheet

>> DEFINE YOUR BUSINESS VALUE PROPOSITION

What does your business sell? Who wants it, and why? In this chapter, you'll sit down and fill out the "business value proposition worksheet." A BVP, or "business value proposition" is a statement that succinctly defines what your business does and the value that it provides to customers. For example, a cupcake bakery bakes yummy cupcakes that people want to eat; a dry cleaner cleans people's dirty clothes; and an automobile insurer provides insurance for people's cars. You produce something that other people want, so what is it?

Define Your Business Value Proposition

One way to define your business value proposition is to look at other companies on the Web, and "reverse engineer" their BVPs.

Here are some more examples, with links to sample websites.

For a New York watch repair shop such as **Ron Gordon Watch Repair** (https://www.rongordonwatches.com/) , the business value proposition is that it provides watch repair services to people living or working in Manhattan who need to get their luxury watches (e.g., Tag Heuer, Breitling, Hamilton) repaired quickly and easily.

For an industrial fan company like **Industrial Fans Direct** (http://www.industrialfansdirect.com/), the business value proposition is to provide quality industrial fans for harsh environments such as factories or farms.

For a San Francisco mortgage broker, such as **Natasha Lovas**, the business value proposition is to help people get cheap mortgages easily. An example website is http://www.san-francisco-mortgage-broker.com/.

For any business, a *business value proposition* is your "elevator pitch" to a potential customer - what do you offer, that they want?

> For your first **TODO**, write a sentence or short paragraph that succinctly defines what your business does and how it provides value for customers. For the **worksheet**, go to https://www.jm-seo.org/workbooks (click on "SEO Fitness 2017," enter the code '2017fitness' to register if you have not already done so), and click on the link to the "business value proposition worksheet."

» IDENTIFY YOUR TARGET CUSTOMERS BY SEGMENT

Your *business value proposition* explicitly describes the relationship between what you sell and what they want. Now dig deeper: *segment* your customers into definable groups. For instance, **Ron Gordon Watch Repair** might segment its customers into the following:

- Manhattan office workers seeking quick and convenient watch repairs on their lunch hours (*Budget and time conscious*).
- Manhattan residents who own stylish, luxury watch brands like Tag Heuer, Breitling, or Rolex watches looking for expert repairs. (*Luxury watch lovers*).
- USA residents who own vintage Zodiac watches who need expert repairs from a watch shop that they trust. (*Vintage watch lovers, nationwide*).

Similarly, a Las Vegas real estate broker might segment his customers by space need – office, warehouse, retail. Moreover, there might be a segmentation based on those looking to rent vs. buy. And a Miami divorce attorney might segment into men vs. women, those with substantial property vs. those without, those who have children vs. those who do not. **A "segment" or "buyer persona" is a group of like-minded customers**.

For your second **TODO**, open up the "business value proposition worksheet" and list **customer segments** – customers who differ by type (income level, geographic location), by need (high end, low end, rent vs. buy), or even geographic location. Try to see your customers as specific groups with specific needs, rather than one amorphous mega group. Begin to think about how each might search Google differently, using different keywords.

» ESTABLISH MARKETING GOALS

Moving from business value proposition and customer segments, it's time to think about definable **goals** or **actions** for your website. For most businesses, a good goal is to get a registration / email address / inquiry in exchange for something free such as a free consult, eBook, or webinar. A Las Vegas real estate company, for instance, might want visitors to the website to "send a message" about their property needs, or register for a free consult with a leasing specialist. Similarly, a divorce attorney might want a potential client to reach out for a free phone consult, and a watch repair shop might just want people to call or email to discuss their watch repair needs, and get directions to the shop.

For most businesses, marketing **goals** on the Web usually boil down to –

- A Website **registration**, **contact form**, or **email via the website** – for a free consult, a software download, a free e-book, a newsletter sign up, etc.
- A **sale** – an e-commerce transaction such as the purchase of a candy gift tin on an e-store, or an iPhone skin via PayPal.

A well-constructed website will lead customers to an easy-to-see first step. Here's a screenshot from http://www.reversemortgage.org/, one of the top websites for the Google search "reverse mortgage," with the goal marked by a red arrow:

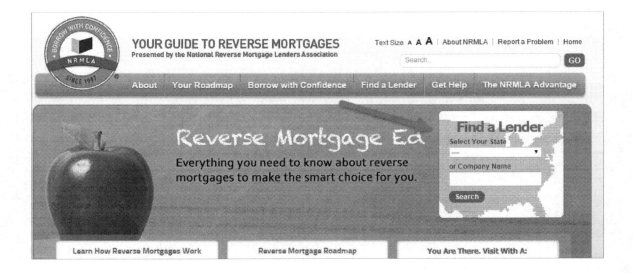

Reversemortgage.org knows what it wants: first, to **rank** at the top of Google search for "reverse mortgage," second, to **get the click**; and third, for a potential customer to start towards the **goal**, i.e. the process of *finding a lender* (and giving the Website his name, email address, and phone number for a sales follow up!).

Abstractly, your process and goals are probably as follows:

1. **Rank high** on a Google search query ("reverse mortgage" in this case).
2. **Get the click** from Google to your website.

3. Once they land, get them to take the "first step" or **"goal"** (usually fill out a feedback form, send an email via the website, or for an eCommerce site to make a first purchase.).
4. **Follow up** with them by email or phone, if necessary, to complete the sales process.

Your Sales Ladder

Defining your next steps or goals of your website is inseparable from defining your **sales ladder**. Web searchers are actively looking for an answer to their query, and they are anything but passive: if they don't see what they want, *click, bounce, bye,* and they're gone.

*(Some marketers talk of a "sales funnel," a concept I do not like because it implies that customers are **passive**, like little marbles that fall into your website and into your registration or sale. I do not think people on the Web (or in life) are passive at all. I think of people as **active** searchers, searching Google, clicking to websites, finding what they want (or not), and being quite skeptical about whether they should take the next action.)*

Customers Are Like Salmon

Let me explain why thinking of customers as jumping "up" a "sales ladder" is a better way to think than "down" a "sales funnel."

I think of *customers* like *salmon* jumping up from sea level in frigid Alaskan rivers, jumping higher and higher up fish ladders (put there by the Alaskan Department of Fish and Game) to get to their goal: the spawning ground. The fish are motivated (*after all, there's mating to be done*), and they are **active** participants in the process. You can't "bait" them with junk either: they need something good at the end of the process.

A good Alaskan fishery expert doesn't engineer one **huge**, **high** jump for the salmon but rather a series of **smaller, easier-to-jump** hurdles that can move the fish from goal one to goal two, etc. Why? Because if the first jump is too high, and too scary, the fish won't make it. Similarly, make your own "first step" non-threatening, and easy!

Make your website goals easy and non-threatening! Don't attempt to go from a website landing to a major purchase; rather break the process into smaller, easier, and less threatening "baby steps." One of the best early steps in your goals is to give away something **free** like a free consultation, free eBook, or free Webinar.

GIVE AWAY SOMETHING FREE IN EXCHANGE FOR CONTACT INFORMATION

Having something **free** (a free webinar, a free consultation, a free e-book) is a tried and true way to make the first step of your ladder easy and non-threatening. People love free, and will give away their email and phone contact information for something free that is also useful. (*From your perspective, this then gives you their email and/or phone number for you and your sales staff to follow up on*). If you are selling something, think of a free sample or money back offer; anything that reduces the risk of making that first buying decision. Using this strategy, make the first step of your sales ladder exciting, enticing, and free!

VIDEO. Watch a video tutorial of the importance of giving away something free on your website at http://jmlinks.com/17p.

Don't Make Customers Think!

Your customers are busy, harried people. The phone is ringing, the baby is crying, the boss is there waiting outside the office as they search Google for products or services. They're busy, multi-tasking people. The design of your website needs to be easy and non-threatening from the perspective of a customer. If you ponder this "as if" you were "inside" the head of the customer, for example, he would be thinking something like the following (using the example of a person who has *international tax problems* and is looking for a CPA or accountant with knowledge of international tax issues):

1. **Customer identifies a need**. "I have income tax issues with respect to international taxes. I need help doing my bookkeeping and preparing my taxes for state, federal, and international tax compliance."
2. **Customer turns to Google**. "I think I'll search Google for 'international tax accountants' in Oklahoma City, OK" (which is where he lives).

3. **Customer refines his keywords**. "I will type into Google searches such as 'international tax CPA,' 'Accountant for International Tax problems OKC', and 'accounting firm overseas taxation in Oklahoma City.'"
4. **Customer browses Google results**. I will browse the first three or four listings on Google (*ignoring the ads*), and click over to the first website at the top of Google.
5. **Customer clicks FROM Google TO each website**. He thinks to himself, "Hm. This looks interesting! They seem to do international taxes, but I don't know...what else is on this website?"
6. **Customer sees a free offer, or first easy step on the sales ladder**. "Oh look, they have a YouTube video that explains their firm, let me watch that."
7. **Customer takes the next easy, non-threatening step on the sales ladder**. "That was pretty good, but oh look, they have a 'free consultation by phone' offer. Let me fill out their feedback form with my name, email address, telephone number, and good time to call."
8. **Customer transitions from the Web to human to human interaction**. Ring, ring. "Who is it?" "Jason McDonald Accountants, we see you are interested in our free 20 minute consult." "Yes, I am... I have these international tax problems... bla, bla, bla." (Conversation with the customer begins).
9. **Customer consummates the sale**. Enough trust has been established, and the customer signs up for the service.

At the end of this process from customer *need* to keyword *search query* to *landing* to *browsing* the website to taking the *easy free actions* such as watching a YouTube video and signing up for a free consultation, hopefully the lead turns into a sale. What you want to do for your own company is take out a piece of paper, and outline steps similar to the ones above. Work backwards from #9 to #1, and customize the process for your own company, product, and/or service.

You will then see that keywords start the process on Google, but the process (hopefully) ends on your website with a sale or sales lead.

Set up a Focus Group

Don't make them think! Don't make your website hard to navigate! Take a moment and look at your web pages from the perspective of a Google searcher. Does it answer a search question? Is the "next step" or "goal" easy to see? Does it look easy or free to take that "next step"" **Don't make customers think!** Don't make customers hunt for goals, or they'll bounce back to Google and be gone.

Indeed, it's a good idea to get friends, family, or others outside your company to come in as a "focus group" and have them look at your website, and attempt to find your goals. If they struggle, you need to revise your website to make it easy. **KISS**: *keep it simple, stupid* is a good motto for effective website design!

If average people can understand your website, and can clearly see the "next step" that they should take like a free consultation, free webinar, or free eBook download, then your website works. If not, you need to redesign it.

Put it All Together

> For your fourth **TODO**, open up your "business value proposition worksheet" and brainstorm your desired web landing next steps or goals (registrations and/or sales) as well as your sales ladder, including the possible use of something "free" to make that first step easy for customers.

For extra credit, begin to think about how you will **measure** these goals. As we will learn in Chapter 6.1, you can use Google Analytics to measure goals such as registrations or sales. But you can also use tactics like special toll-free 800 numbers, vanity phone extensions, and offer codes to track whether someone is coming from a Web search to a phone call into your call center.

Goals and measurability go hand-in-hand.

》》 DELIVERABLE: A COMPLETED BUSINESS VALUE PROPOSITION WORKSHEET

Now that we've come to the end of Step 1.2, you should have your **DELIVERABLE** ready: a completed **business value proposition worksheet**. This worksheet should define your business value proposition, customer segments, search paths, desired next steps (goals) and your sales ladder, and even how you plan to measure customer progress along the sales ladder. In Chapter 2.1, we will turn to defining your keywords (which builds upon this knowledge), but first let's turn to the "big picture" of how SEO works.

SURVEY OFFER

CLAIM YOUR $10 REBATE OR FREE BOOK! HERE'S HOW –

4. Visit http://jmlinks.com/survey.
5. Take a short, simple survey about the book.
6. Indicate whether you want a $10.00 rebate or a free copy of one of Jason's other books on SEO / Social Media Marketing / Job Search & Career-building.

WE WILL THEN –

- Rebate you the $10.00, or send you a free copy of one of the other books.

~ $10 REBATE OFFER ~

~ LIMITED TO ONE PER CUSTOMER ~

EXPIRES: 3/1/2017

SUBJECT TO CHANGE WITHOUT NOTICE

GOT QUESTIONS? CALL 800-298-4065

1.3
BASICS

I like to think of SEO like a **game**, a competitive game like running a marathon, playing poker, or another competitive endeavor in life: **the art and science of getting a job**. Every game has its rules, of course, and if you don't know the rules of the game, you surely can't win. A good way to understand the "game" of SEO is to compare it to the process of getting a job. It has its **job desired** (your *keywords*), its **resume** (your *website*), its **references** (your inbound *links*), and its job **interview** (your website *landing*).

In this Chapter, I will give you a *conceptual framework* to understand search engine optimization. Once you have a conceptual framework, you can then refer back to it, as you dive into very specific tasks such as optimizing a landing page or soliciting inbound links. It's a map that will keep you oriented in the right direction.

Let's get started!

TODO LIST:

>> Understand that SEO Parallels Getting a Job

>> Keyword Research

>> Understand "On Page" SEO

>> Understand "Off Page" SEO

>> Set Landing Page Goals

>> UNDERSTAND THAT SEO PARALLELS GETTING A JOB

Let's consider the search for a job. How does the job market work? People want to "be found" as the "ideal" candidate for a position. So what do they do? Four important things:

Job Desired – Identify a Desired Job. Job seekers take a look inside their souls and identify the job they want. If they're smart, they took a look outside at the job market as well, and look for connection points between the job of their dreams, and the jobs that are in demand in the labor market. For example, my dream job is sipping margaritas in Puerta Vallarta, Mexico, writing science fiction novels, but the demand for that isn't so high. So I've taken a passion for language and turned that into a job as an SEO writer and consultant. Notice how the "job desired" matches "keywords" as in (*SEO consultant*).

Resume - Create a resume. Job seekers create a keyword-heavy **resume** that explains the job that they want to get, and their qualifications for that job. If, for example, they want a job as a BMW auto mechanic, they create a resume that emphasizes keywords like "auto mechanic," "auto repair," and even "BMW repair" by prominently displaying them in the right places, including the subject line of emails they send out to prospective employers. And employers "scan" resumes looking for those resumes that "match" their keywords. Notice how "keywords" are embedded in the written resume.

References - Cultivate References. Beyond a great resume, the next aspect of job search is cultivating great **references**. Knowing the boss's wife, having the head of the BMW auto mechanic school, or someone else important or influential, put in a good word can elevate your resume to the top of the heap. In short, strong references get your resume looked at, substantiate that your resume is factually accurate, and possibly get you a job interview. Notice how "references" are external validations that you are as great as your resume claims you to be.

Job Interview – Wow Them Face-to-Face. Once you get their attention, what's next? The job **interview** is the next step towards landing the job, it's the "free glimpse" of what you have to offer that "sells" the employer on making a financial commitment by hiring you. Notice how a "job interview" is a "free" taste of you as an employee. The use of something **free** is obvious, *once you notice it*, and notice how strong websites usually offer customers something **free** as well.

The **marketing equation** is: **job desired** > **resume** > **references** > **job interview** > **job**.

Hopefully you can already see that SEO is a lot like getting a job. How so?

Identifying the job you want equals identifying keywords that are in demand. Before you put virtual pen to virtual paper to build out your website, you have to understand your Business Value Proposition, and who wants what you have to sell. "Keywords" connect what you have, with what customers want. This is called "**keyword research.**"

Creating a resume equals creating a strong, keyword heavy website. Your website, in a sense, is your business resume, and it needs to have keywords placed on it in strategic places to "talk to" Google as well as human searchers, and just as with a job search, you have to research the hot button keywords that people are searching for and place those in strategic positions. This is called "**on page**" SEO.

Cultivating references equals getting links and going social. Just as you cultivate references to get your resume elevated to the top of the heap, so you cultivate inbound links, fresh buzz, and social mentions to elevate your website to the top of Google search. Getting other websites to link to you, and social media sites like Google+ or Twitter to mention your website, is called "**off page**" SEO.

The job interview equals the website landing. Once you get noticed, your next step is a fantastic job interview. The equivalent of the job interview is the **landing behavior** on your website. Once they land from Google, you want them to "take the next step," usually a registration or a sale just as at a job interview, which leads to the final step, getting hired or making a sale.

The **SEO equation** is **keyword research** > **on page SEO** > **off page SEO** > **website landing** > **sales inquiry** or **sale**.

Keep this conceptual framework that SEO is like job search in the back of your head as you read through this Workbook. Here's a simple model of the parallels:

job desired = keywords = identify keywords that customers search for

resume = "on page" SEO = create a keyword heavy, easy-to-understand website

references = "off page" SEO = solicit many inbound links, social authority / mentions, and freshness via blogging

job interview = optimize the "landing page experience" to lead to a registration or a sale.

Can it be that simple? Yes.

Do most people have bad resumes? Yes.

Do most people have bad websites? Yes.

Does that mean that your resume, or website, has to be bad? No.

Indeed, the fact that most people do SEO badly actually means that it is a <u>huge opportunity</u> for you and your company.

A few simple changes such as placing your keywords into strategic positions on your website can have a huge impact!

You don't have to run faster than the bear, just faster than your buddy!

Your website, just like your resume, does **NOT** have to be **perfect**. It just has to be **BETTER** than that of your competition. And your competition is not made of Albert Einsteins and Madame Curies, but just regular guys and gals most of whom probably know less about SEO than you do.

>> KEYWORD RESEARCH

Let's drill down into the first element, "keyword research," the equivalent of identifying a job that you want that's also in demand in the marketplace. We'll get into some cool tactics and tools in Chapter Two, but for now, here are the steps:

1. Write down your Business Value Proposition, with an eye to the "words" that "describe" what you have that people want.
2. Look for "words" that connect "what you sell" with what "customers want."
3. Brainstorm how customers might search Google to find your company, product or service.
4. Write down a "keyword list" with special attention to those keywords that are really, really hot matches connecting a customer who's "ready to buy" with "what you have to sell."

At the end of this process, you'll have a list of keywords that your customers type into Google.

» "On Page" SEO

Let's drill down into the second element, "on page" SEO, the equivalent of a great resume. What are the steps? We'll assume that you have your keyword list in hand; that is, you know "which job" you want, or in SEO terms, which keywords you want to optimize for. Once you know your keywords, where do you put them?

In terms of "on page" SEO, the main places you put your keywords are as follows:

Page Tags. Place your keywords strategically in the right page tags, beginning with the TITLE tag on each page, followed by the header tag family, image alt attribute, and HTML cross-links from one page to another on your site.

Keyword Density. Write keyword-heavy copy for your web pages, and pay attention to writing quality. Complying to Google's *Panda* update means placing your keywords into grammatically correct sentences, and making sure that your writing contains similar and associated words vs. your keyword targets.

Home Page SEO. Use your home page wisely, by placing keywords in relatively high density on your home page and, again, in natural syntax, as well as creating "one click" links from your home page to your subordinate pages.

Website structure. Organize your website to be Google friendly, starting with keyword-heavy URLS, cross-linking with keyword text, and using sitemaps and other Google-friendly tactics.

"On page" SEO is all about knowing your keywords and building keyword-heavy content that communicates your priorities to Google just as a good resume communicates your job search priorities to prospective employers. We'll investigate "on page" SEO more deeply in Chapters Three and Four.

» "Off Page" SEO

Let's drill down into the third element, "off page" SEO, the equivalent of great references. Here, you do not fully control the factors that help you with Google (unlike in "on page" SEO), so the game is played out in how well you can convince others to talk favorably about you and your website. Paralleling job references, the main strategic factors of "off page" SEO are as follows:

Link Building. As we shall see, links are the votes of the Web. Getting as many qualified websites to link back to your website, especially high authority websites as ranked (secretly) by Google, using keyword-heavy syntax, is what link building is all about. It's that simple, and that complicated.

Social Authority / Mentions. Social media is the new buzz of the Internet, and Google looks for mentions of your website on social sites like Google+, Twitter, and Facebook as well as how robust your own profiles are.

Freshness. Like a prospective employer, Google rewards sites that show fresh activity. "What have you done lately?" is a common job interview question, and in SEO you need to communicate to Google that you are active via frequent content updates such as blog posts and press releases.

"Off page" SEO is all about building external links to your site just as getting good references is all about cultivating positive buzz about you as a potential employee. We'll investigate "off page" SEO more deeply in Chapter Five. Oh, and due to the recent Google algorithm change called *Penguin*, we'll emphasize that you want to cultivate *natural* inbound links as opposed to *artificial* links that scream "manipulation" at Google! It's good *believable* references that help you in a job search, and, post-*Penguin*, it's good *believable* links that help you with SEO.

▶ SET LANDING PAGE GOALS

Let's drill down into the fourth element, "Landing Page Goals," the equivalent of great job interview skills. The point of a great website isn't just to get traffic from Google, after all. It's to move that potential customer up your sales ladder – from website landing to a registration for something free (a "sales lead") or perhaps even a sale.

So in evaluating your website, you want to evaluate each and every page and each and every page element for one variable: do they move customers up the **sales ladder**? Is the **desired action** (*registration* or *sale*) clearly visible on each page, and if so, is it enticing to the customer usually with something free like a free download, free consult, free webinar and the like?

Just as after a job interview, your family and friends ask whether you "got the job," after a Web landing you are asking yourself whether it "got the action" such as a registration or a sale. Web traffic just like sending out resumes is not an end in itself, but a means to an end!

VIDEO. Watch a video tutorial on the basics of SEO explained in "plain English" at http://jmlinks.com/17k.

We shall now explore each of these topics in-depth.

2.1
KEYWORDS

If Step #1 is "Set the Right Expectations," Step #2 is to define your **keywords**. Customers start their quest to "find you" by typing in **keywords** or **key phrases** into Google, Yahoo, or Bing. (For simplicity's sake, I'll use the word *keyword* to mean either a *single* or *multi-word* phrase as a search engine query). Identifying **customer-centric keywords** is the foundation of effective SEO. Your best keywords match your **business value proposition** with **high volume, high value keywords** used by your customers.

- In **Step 2.1**, we'll brainstorm our list of keywords, focusing on "getting all the words" on paper as a **keyword brainstorm** document.
- In **Step 2.2**, we'll turn to organizing these keywords into a structured **keyword worksheet**.

For now, don't worry about how to organize your keywords. Your goal in this Chapter is to get **all** your possible keyword targets on paper; this Chapter is about brainstorming your keyword universe.

Let's get started!

TODO LIST:

» Brainstorm Your Keywords

» Reverse Engineer Competitors' Keywords

» Use Google Tricks to Identify Possible Keywords

» Use the Google AdWords Keyword Planner

»» Deliverable: Keyword Brainstorm Worksheet

❯❯ BRAINSTORM YOUR KEYWORDS

Sit down in a quiet place with a good cup of coffee or tea, or if you prefer, a martini, i.e. *anything to get your ideas flowing*! Brainstorm the **keywords** that a customer might type into Google that are relevant to your company, your product, and/or your service.

> *When a potential customer sits down at Google, what words do they type in?*
>
> *Which keywords are DEFINITELY those of your customers?*
>
> *Which keywords are CLOSE to a decision to buy? Which are farther away, earlier in the sales ladder?*
>
> *Which customer segments use which keywords, and how might keywords differ among your customer segments?*
>
> *Which keywords match which product or service lines as produced by your company?*

Conduct a Keyword Brainstorming Session

I highly recommend that you organize a formal keyword brainstorming session with your marketing team (it might be just you by yourself, or it might be your CEO, your marketing manager, and a few from the sales staff). Devote at least ONE HOUR to brainstorming keywords; close the door, turn off the cell phone, tell your secretary to "hold all calls" and start drinking (either coffee or martinis).

> *Brainstorm, brainstorm, brainstorm the keywords that customers are typing into Google. Try not to miss any possible keyword combinations!*
>
> *Do this, first, individually – take out a piece of paper, and write keyword ideas down WITHOUT talking to the others in your group.*
>
> *Don't be shy. Don't leave anything out. The goal is to get EVERYTHING on paper, no matter how ridiculous it might be.*
>
> *Then have a group session and go over all the keywords each person has identified.*

Drink some more coffee, or more martinis, and keep brainstorming – write all possible keywords on a white board, a piece of paper, or a Word / Google document.

Don't censor yourself because there are no wrong answers. The goal of this exercise is to get the complete "universe" of all possible keywords that customers might type into Google.

"Think like a customer" sitting at his or her computer screen at Google:

- **Assume you are a completely new, novice customer**. Assume you know next to nothing. What single words or multi-word phrases (keywords) would you type into Google?
- **Segment your customers into different groups**. What keywords might each group use, and how would they differ from other groups?
- **Are there are any specific "helper" words that a potential customer might use?** Common helper words specify geographic locality (e.g., San Francisco, Berkeley, San Jose), for example. Others specify things like "free," "cheap," "trial," or "information."
- **Don't miss your synonyms!** If you are a "lawyer," don't miss "attorney." If you are a "dry cleaner," don't miss "wash and fold" or "laundry service." If you are an "SEO expert," don't miss "SEO consultant." If you are an orthopedic surgeon, don't miss "knee doctor."

For your first **TODO**, open up the "keyword brainstorm worksheet" in either Word or PDF, and begin to fill it out as completely as possible. For the worksheet, go to https://www.jm-seo.org/workbooks (click on "SEO Fitness 2017," and enter the code '2017fitness' to register if you have not already done so), and click on the link to the "keyword brainstorm worksheet."

Again, for right now, don't worry about the *organization* of your keywords. Don't police your thoughts. Write down every word that comes to mind - synonyms, competitor names, misspellings, alternative word orders. Let your mind wander. This is the keyword discovery phase, so don't exclude anything!

>> REVERSE ENGINEER COMPETITORS

After you've completed this first wave of brainstorming, let's you and your group members do some searches on Google for target keywords. Take a few of the keywords you've already identified, and type them into Google. As you search Google, identify your "Google competitors," that is, companies that are on page one of the Google results and therefore doing well in terms of SEO. You'll want to **reverse engineer** their keywords.

Here's how.

First, click over to their home page or whatever page is showing up on page one of Google for a search that matters to you. Next, view the HTML source code of this page. To do this, in Firefox and Chrome, use *right click*, then **V**iew, **P**age Source. In Internet Explorer, use **V**iew, **S**ource on the file menu. Finally, find the following tags in the HTML source code:

```
<Title>
<Meta Name="Description" Content="...">
<Meta Name="Keywords" Content="...">
```

If you have trouble finding these HTML tags, use CTRL+F (on a PC vs. Command+F on a Mac) on your keyboard, and in the dialog box type *<title, description,* or *keywords*

For each, write down those keywords your competitor has identified that might also be applicable to you. Here's a screenshot of http://www.globalindustrial.com/c/hvac/fans, one of the top Google performers for the search "industrial fans" with the three critical tags highlighted in yellow -

```
13
14
15
16
17  <!DOCTYPE html PUBLIC "-//W3C//DTD XHTML 1.0 Transitional//EN" "http://ww
18  <html xmlns="http://www.w3.org/1999/xhtml" xml:lang="en" lang="en">
19    <head>
20      <meta http-equiv="Content-Type" content="text/html; charset=iso-8859-
21      <meta http-equiv="Content-Language" content="en-us"/>
22      <title>Pedestal Fans | Agricultural Fans | Blower Fans | Ceiling Fans
23
24      <meta name="category" content="Fans"/>
25
26      <meta name="keywords" content="Fans - Agricultural, Loading Dock, Ped
    Styles & Sizes At Global Industria"/>
27
28      <meta name="description" content="Pedestal Fans - Agricultural Fans,
    From Hundreds Of Styles & Sizes At Global Industrial"/>
29
30
31
32
```

Read each tag out loud to your group members. Notice how each tag in the source reveals the "thought process" behind this page, showing the synonyms "fan" for "blower," plus the "types" of fans people might search for - pedestal, agricultural, ceiling, etc. The goal of viewing the source of your competitors' pages is to "steal" their keyword ideas, and write down any relevant keywords onto your "keyword brainstorm" document.

> **VIDEO.** Watch a quick video tutorial on how to use "view source" to reverse engineer competitors at http://jmlinks.com/5k.

For your second **TODO**, open up your "keyword brainstorm worksheet," and jot down the top five competitors who appear at the top of Google for your target keywords, use the tactic above to view their source, and then write down keyword ideas taken from their TITLE, META DESCRIPTION, and META KEYWORDS tags.

Did you discover any keywords you left out in your first brainstorming session? If so, be sure to write those on your list.

>> Use Google Tricks to Identify Possible Keywords

After you have brainstormed keywords and used View Source to view the keywords of competitors, it's time to use free Google tools for keyword discovery. You can find a complete list in the companion *SEO Toolbook* (*Keywords Chapter*) or on my SEO dashboard (both available at http://jmlinks.com/seodash), but here are my favorite strategies starting with Google's own free tools.

First, simply go to Google and start typing your keyword. Pay attention to the pull down menu that automatically appears. This is called **Google Suggest** or **Autocomplete** and is based on actual user queries. It's a quick and easy way to find "helper" words for any given search phrase. You can also place a space (hit your space bar) after your target keyword, and then go through the alphabet typing "a", "b", etc.

Here's a screenshot of **Google Suggest** using the key phrase "motorcycle insurance"

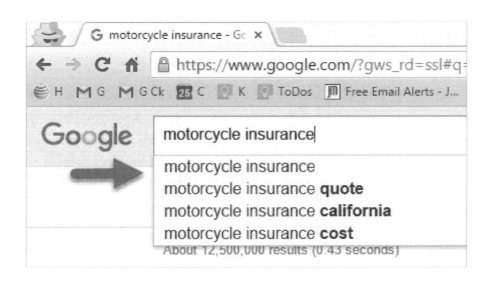

Hit your space key after the last letter of the last keyword (e.g., after *motorcycle insurance*) and more keyword suggestions appear. You can also type the letters of the alphabet – a, b, c, etc. and Google will give you suggestions. Here's a screenshot for the letter "b":

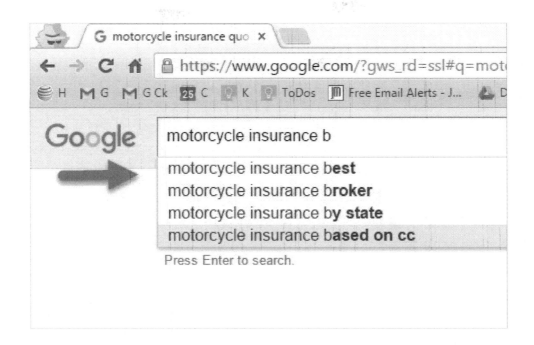

Second, type in one of your target keyword phrases and scroll to the bottom of the Google search page. Google will often give you **related searches** based on what people often search on after their original search. Here's a screen shot for "motorcycle insurance" -

Searches related to motorcycle insurance

cheap motorcycle insurance	how much is motorcycle insurance
cheapest motorcycle insurance	motorcycle insurance comparison
motorcycle insurance rates	motorcycle insurance cost
best motorcycle insurance	average motorcycle insurance

Note the **helper words** it tells you people use to search: cheap, rates, best, "how much," comparison, cost, and average. Are these not wonderful clues as to how customers search Google? As you look at Google autocomplete and related searches, add these keywords to your master list.

Ubersuggest

A third party tool that pulls data from Bing search queries is Ubersuggest at https://ubersuggest.io/. It basically types through the alphabet for you, and gives you nifty keywords. Spend some quality time with the Google tools as well as Ubersuggest.org, using your "starter" keywords and looking for synonyms and helper words.

> **VIDEO.** Watch a quick video tutorial on how to use Google autocomplete and related searches to generate keyword ideas at http://jmlinks.com/18n.

These three Google tricks are great ways to find helper words, related phrases, and synonyms for your target keywords and key phrases. For your third **TODO**, open up your "keyword brainstorm worksheet" and write down some keyword ideas garnered from these free tools. You want a messy, broad and complete list of the "universe" of possible customer keywords via your own brainstorming process, via reverse engineering your competitors, and now via Google tools such as autocomplete and related searches.

» USE THE GOOGLE ADWORDS KEYWORD PLANNER

Now it's time to use the most comprehensive keyword tool of them all: Google's own official **AdWords Keyword Planner.** It's free, but you'll need an AdWords account to use it fully.

> **VIDEO.** Watch two quick video tutorials on how to use the Google AdWords Keyword Planner *in general* at http://jmlinks.com/17j and *to brainstorm keywords* at http://jmlinks.com/18m.

Sign up for AdWords

To sign up for AdWords, go to http://adwords.google.com/. You'll need a credit card to set up an account, and the Google interface will attempt to get you to start advertising right away. (*You're not actually going to advertise; you're just getting around Google's restrictions on how to access the Keyword Planner*).

AdWords will FORCE you to set up your first campaign, with groups, ads, and keywords. Simply follow their instructions "as if" you were going to set up an ad, and immediately set your first campaign to "pause." To pause your campaign, follow the AdWords set-up instructions to set up your account and then click on the "campaigns" tab, select the checkbox to the left of your first campaign, click "edit" in the menu, and then "pause." (You can even call AdWords at 866-246-6453 and ask them for help on how to set up your advertising campaigns, and then *sneakily* ask them to **pause your campaigns** – just explain that you are just setting things up, right now, and you do not want to turn on any advertising at this time). If you're worried about credit card fraud, just go to your local grocery card and get a "gift card" with the VISA logo to set up your AdWords account. The point of all this is to use a credit card to set up an active AdWords account, and then use this account to access the Keyword Planner.

New for 2017: Google Goes Evil

As of late 2016, Google is now requiring that you spend money to get accurate data out of the Keyword Planner. Sadly, Google as a monopoly is acting as a monopoly and refusing to provide accurate keyword data to those who do not have established AdWords accounts spending money. In my opinion, this is a violation of the public trust the Google has as a near monopoly on search, but absent government regulation, it's Google's world – we just live in it!

Accordingly, you may need to allocate a few hundred dollars and run some actual ads before you'll get accurate keyword information out of the tool. Alternatively, some good competitive tools are the Bing Webmaster Tools' Keyword Tool (http://jmlinks.com/19g), the SERPS.com keyword tool (http://jmlinks.com/19e) and Google's global market finder (http://jmlinks.com/19f).

> **VIDEO.** Watch a video tutorial on alternatives to the Google AdWords Keyword Planner at http://jmlinks.com/19d.

I know it's a bit of a pain, but once you have an operational AdWords account, you can use the Google AdWords Keyword Planner as a wonderful way to research SEO keywords, and you don't have to ever actually advertise. Let's return to the Keyword Planner.

Use the AdWords Keyword Planner Tool to Identify SEO Keywords

Now that you're signed in to your AdWords account, next, go to the "Tools" tab at the top, and scroll down to "Keyword Planner." Here's a screenshot:

Here's how to use it.

First, get past the "welcome screen" by typing your keywords underneath "Search for new keywords using a phrase, website or category" and hitting the blue "Get Ideas" button. This will get you into the actual tool. Here's a screenshot:

This gets you into the tool's real interface. This is where you'll do most of your work, and it looks like this:

A note to the wise: The Keyword Planner is not going to go down in Google history as the best-designed user interface! To be blunt, Google has done a pretty terrible job with the user interface but because of Google's search dominance it remains the data source for keyword research. Google has the data, and you have to master the Keyword Planner! Just be patient, and click around on the tool to learn its operation and secrets.

For purposes of our example, let's assume we are a New York orthopedic surgeon specializing in knee surgery, and so we'll enter "knee pain." After you click "get ideas," you'll see a tab called "Ad group ideas," and one called "keyword ideas." Scroll down under the "ad group" ideas and click "into" the various suggested groups. Google will give you good ideas for related keywords here. For instance, if you type in "knee surgeons," Google will give you these suggestions:

Ad group ideas	Keyword ideas

Ad group (by relevance)

Knee Surgeons (20) knee surgeons, knee replacement surgeons,...	〜
Best Knee (11) best knee surgeons, best knee replacement ...	〜
Cost Knee (13) knee replacement cost, knee replacement s...	〜
Orthopedic Surgeons (33) orthopedic surgeon, orthopedic surgeons, ort...	〜
Knee Arthroscopy (7) knee arthroscopy, arthroscopy knee, arthros...	〜
Orthopedic Doctors (30) orthopedic doctors, orthopedic doctor, what i...	〜
Reconstruction (7) knee reconstruction, acl reconstruction, kne...	〜

Click on any group, and Google will drill down into more related searches. All of these give you great ideas for possible keywords. Note that it also gives you volume information; a rough approximation for how frequently a keyword phrase is actually used.

Don't Miss Your Synonyms!

Notice how the tool gives you both *helper* words and *synonyms*. For example, you get *best* knee replacement, telling you that *best* is a helper word, and you get *doctor* as well as *surgeon*, *orthopedic* as well as *knee*. The tool is telling you how people search: some people search for *knee doctors*, and others for *orthopedic surgeons*. Many people search for *best* knee surgeons (and to the contrary, few search for *worst* knee surgeons). Because to Google *a word is just a word*, you want to be sure to capture ALL your key synonyms. A search for "best knee doctor in San Francisco" is different from a search for "best orthopedic surgeon in San Francisco," even though the latter may include the former, i.e. many people searching for orthopedic surgeons who do knees. This is true across all domains; a *lawyer*, to Google, is not the same as an *attorney*. In summary be sure to identify all your helpers and synonyms, and write these down on your Keyword Brainstorm Worksheet.

Next, click on the tab "Keyword ideas," you should see something like:

Keyword (by relevance)		Avg. monthly searches [?]
knee surgeons	⌁	320
best knee surgeons	⌁	210
knee replacement surgeons	⌁	140
top knee surgeons	⌁	210
best knee replacement surgeons	⌁	390
best knee surgeon	⌁	90
knee surgery	⌁	18,100
knee replacement	⌁	60,500

Again, Google is giving you great ideas of related or helper words (e.g. "best") as well as synonyms (e.g., "knee replacement" for "knee surgery"). Note the ones down that make sense, and write them onto your keyword brainstorm worksheet.

Next, you'll want to play around with the tool and understand some of its more advanced features. Let's start with the columns and pull-outs mean. Starting on the left column, take a look at "Targeting." You'll see here it will default to "All locations" or perhaps "United States." If you click the pencil to the right of "United States," you can drill down to specific states or even cities by typing their names into this space and then clicking "remove" on other entries. This is useful if you'd like to know keyword search volume for specific states; at the city level, the tool isn't very useful as the search volume is often insufficient, however. Alternatively, you can "remove" the United States and target "All locations" which is "Google speak" for the entire world. Note that to activate a change just click elsewhere on the screen or hit enter. (The brilliant engineers at Google failed to clarify how to enter data into the tool!)

Generally speaking, you'll need a broad geography: so choose "United States" rather than "Tulsa, Oklahoma" to research "industrial fans" or "knee surgeons" as you brainstorm keywords. If a search is too narrow, the tool returns zero data.

The **Negative keywords** feature also has some utility. You can filter "out" keywords that don't matter to you. For example, if we type in "exercises" it then filters out keyword phrases that contain the word "exercises." Many companies want to filter out words like "free" or "cheap," so use negative keywords for any desired refinement.

Columns. On the middle of the page, find the Columns button and click on the downward chevron. Here's a screenshot:

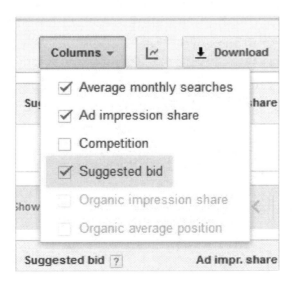

Be sure to click the box next to "Suggested bid" as you definitely want this one to show.

We'll discuss what "suggested bid" means in a moment, but basically it's the average amount competitors are willing to pay Google to get a click from Google to their website via AdWords advertising. I think of it like the "price per pound" of fish at the fish market.

If the "suggested bid" is $2.99 for "knee pain" this means advertisers are willing to pay Google $2.99 for each and every click FROM Google TO their website.

Refocusing the Keyword Planner

You may notice that the tool gives you very broad and often irrelevant keyword suggestions, so I often recommend that you refocus it to just your target phrase and related phrases. To do this, on the left-hand column where it says "Keyword Options," click there, and then select "Only show ideas closely related to my search terms" by moving the blue button to "on" and clicking on the blue "save" button. Here's a screenshot:

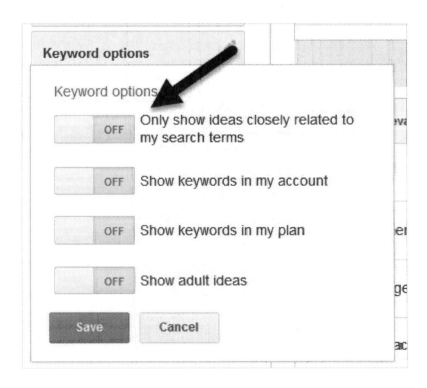

Once you click "off" to "on" for "Only show ideas closely related to my search terms," you've reset the Keyword Planner to zero in on more specific keywords. Once you've done that, you should see something like this:

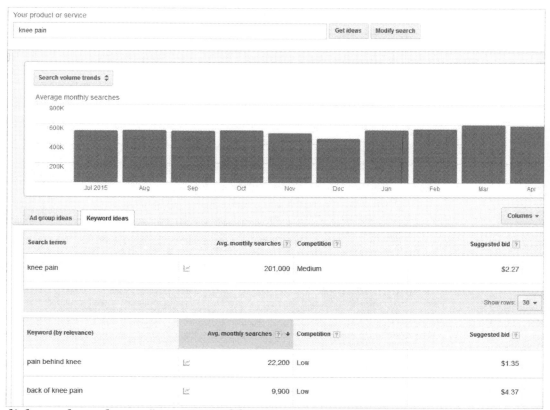

Now click on the column "Avg. monthly searches," and the tool will sort your keywords by volume (the number of searches per month for your target geography). The above screenshot is for "knee pain" after having focused the tool by entering "knee pain" with location set to "all locations," and "Keyword filters" set to "Only show ideas closely related to my search terms":

You can see the average monthly search volume for "knee pain" for "all locations" is 110,000. The number 1 phrase is "pain behind knee" at 22,200 followed by "back of knee pain" at 14,800. **Note that these search volumes refer to exact match only: they take into account only when a searcher enters that phrase and nothing more.** For example, 8,100 people entered "back of knee pain" and no additional words. Similarly, 110,000 people entered the phrase "knee pain" in the last thirty days and <u>no additional words</u>. If they enter "sharp knee pain" that does NOT count in this total.

(**Note**: the volumes you see may differ from the above, or you may see a "range" of volumes if you have not spent enough money in AdWords. Take all the volumes in the tool as illustrations only – despite Google's public brand persona, the tool seems to be incredibly inaccurate! Use it more to get a sense of range, which keywords are more popular than others as opposed to a scientific treatise on actual keyword volumes).

If you'd like to drill down to a phrase, then you have to re-enter it in the top. Enter "back of knee pain" and Google will give you the related helper words such as "pain behind knee cap," "sharp pain behind knee, etc."

Unfortunately, the Keyword Planner gives only "exact match" data, so you have to manually enter a bunch of related keyword phrases and then tally them up to get a total for phrases.

The Keyword Planner has been strongly criticized by the SEO community for this flaw, because the old Keyword Tool did allow such functionality, but to no avail. So, so far you can only get keyword volumes for exact match. And, the data that it does provide seems to be rather inaccurate. So for now, to compare keyword volumes you are left with manually "guessing" related phrase and entering them into the tool.

You can, however, enter multiple phrases and compare them. Let's set our location to New York, NY, and let's take these keywords:

> *knee pain*
> *knee surgery*
> *knee surgeon*
> *knee surgeons New York*

To compare phrases, enter them as a <u>comma separated phrase</u> as follows and click "Get ideas":

> *knee pain, knee surgery, knee surgeon, knee surgeons New York*

Here's a screenshot:

Keyword Volume vs. Value

To understand what this all means, let's use an analogy: **fishing** and **fish**. As the SEO technician, you're the **fisherman** of course.

First, you want to "fish where the fish are." This is the column "Avg. monthly searches" showing you that there are 4,400 searches in New York, NY, for "knee pain" vs. only 20 for "knee surgeon" and even fewer for "knee surgeons New York." However, you want to catch yummy fish and the price per pound as set by the market gives you a strong clue as to their value: *tilapia* at $1.00 a pound isn't as tasty as organic *halibut* at $22.00 a pound. Similarly, *knee pain* is worth only $2.60 per click, while *knee surgeon* is worth $9.07.

Volume vs. Value

There is, in short, a see-saw between **volume** (*fish where the fish are*) and **value** (*catch yummy fish*); the AdWords marketplace is telling you that "knee surgeon" is worth MORE than "knee pain" even though "knee surgeon" has far less volume.

Why? Well, think about what each search query tells you about the customer need.

A search for "knee pain" might be someone who needs an aspirin (a $1.00 sale at best), while a search for "knee surgeon" is probably someone who is looking for surgery (easily $50,000).

"Knee pain" is an "educational" search by someone who is using Google to learn vs. "knee surgeon," which is a "transactional" search by someone who is using Google to find a surgeon to buy knee surgery from.

In general, "educational" searches will have lower average costs-per-click indicating lesser value that "transactional" searches; AdWords is giving you strong clues as to "where the fish are," and "which fish are yummy to eat."

Your competitors using AdWords, in short, are bidding up the keywords that are likely to end in sales and thus telling you which keywords you should SEO!

More on Educational vs. Transactional Keywords

Another way to look at this is that keywords that are *early* in the sales ladder occur usually when a person is just learning, just educating himself about an issue and not likely to buy something. These are called **educational keywords** and generally have low cost-per-click in AdWords. Keywords that occur *late* in the sales ladder are when they are looking to buy something, or make an engagement. These are called **transactional keywords** and generally have high cost-per-click in AdWords. In general, you want to optimize for transactional keywords if possible.

VIDEO. Watch a quick video tutorial on distinguishing educational vs. transactional keywords, volume vs. value at http://jmlinks.com/18k. .

You're **best SEO** occurs at focused, transactional keywords, not educational keywords. You're looking for the "sweet spot" between volume and value, education and transaction.

Let me emphasize this:

Identify and optimize for transactional, late stage, high value keywords.

I, Jason McDonald, do not want to be at the top of Google for "SEO." But I do want to be at the top of Google for "SEO Expert San Francisco." Why? Because the former is an early stage, low value educational search, while the latter is a late stage, high value transactional search: someone who wants to hire me as a high-paid consultant.

A knee surgeon wants to be at the top of Google for "San Francisco Knee Surgeons" and not for "knee pain," because the former are potential patients looking for knee surgery and the latter could be practically anyone with a sore knee and just needing an aspirin.

That said, you still need to rely on your instinct to determine your best keywords and then bolster that with real data from your Google Analytics, which we discuss in the last chapter. The Keyword Planner is only a tool, and the art of SEO still means a lot of head-scratching to identify those keywords that are not just high volume but also high value.

Riches are in the Niches

Back to fishing, if you want to "fish where the fish are" (*high volume keywords*) and "catchy yummy fish" (*high value keywords*), you also want to find "secret fishing holes." These are keyword phrases that tend to yield good customers <u>yet your competitors have not discovered</u>. They are less expensive in AdWords, and easier to optimize for via SEO (because they are undiscovered). If you discover a "secret fishing hole" vs. one everyone knows about, you have struck gold (to mix metaphors). Don't tell anyone! **Riches**, in sum, are in the **niches** when it comes to keywords and SEO.

For "knee pain," the niche search is "knee surgeon" or better yet, "best knee surgeons in the Bay Area."

Here's another example. Let's assume you sell *auto insurance*. The generic "auto insurance" keyword query will have a lot of volume, and a lot of value, and be pretty difficult to show up high on Google for because of intense competition. In this case, look for "niche" keywords such as "auto insurance for teens," or "auto insurance for high risk drivers," or even "auto insurance for classic cars." You may find that highly profitable niches of your business reflect highly profitable keyword queries for SEO, and – to the extent that your competitors are ignorant – a "secret" niche keyword is the best of all.

Get ALL Your Keyword Ideas Down on Paper

For your final **TODO**, open up your "keyword brainstorm worksheet," and jot down keyword volumes and the CPC values of relevant keywords. Again, don't worry about being organized. Just indicate – in general – which keywords are higher volume vs. higher value, which ones are educational vs. transactional. It won't be a perfect map, but you will start to see patterns as to volume and value.

≫≫ DELIVERABLE: A COMPLETED KEYWORD BRAINSTORM WORKSHEET

Now we've come to the end of Step 2.1, and you should have the chapter **DELIVERABLE** ready: your completed **keyword brainstorm worksheet**.

Remember the "Keyword Brainstorm" document will be messy. Its purpose is to get all relevant keywords, helper words, and keyword ideas about volume and value down on paper. In Step 2.2, we will turn to **organizing** our keywords into a structured **keyword worksheet**.

2.2

KEYWORD WORKSHEET

Now that you have a keyword **brainstorm document**, it's time to get organized! Step #2.2 is all about taking the *disorganized* list of keywords and turning them into an *organized*, structured **keyword worksheet** that reflects your keyword **search patterns** as well as **volume** and **value**. You'll use your keyword worksheet as your "SEO blueprint" for many tasks, such as measuring your rank on Google, structuring your website to tell Google what keywords matter to you, writing better blog posts and so on. In my method of doing SEO, I emphasize that it is <u>absolutely essential</u> that your company create and use a keyword worksheet to guide your SEO efforts.

Do not skip this step!

The **DELIVERABLES** for Step 2.2 are your **keyword worksheet** as well as a **rank measurement / baseline** of where your website ranks for target keywords searches on Google.

Let's get started!

TODO LIST:

» Identify Your Main Keyword Structural Patterns

» Create Your Keyword Worksheet

» » Deliverable: Your Keyword Worksheet

» Measure Your Google Rank vs. Keywords

» » Deliverable: Rank Measurement and a Baseline Score

After you complete your **keyword brainstorm** worksheet, your head may be spinning (*especially if you and your team were using martinis rather than coffee as the drink of choice during the brainstorm exercise*). Now it's time to shift gears and to organize those keywords into "structural patterns" with an eye to both keyword volume and value.

Here's where we're going:

> **Brainstorm** *your keywords >* **organize** *them into a keyword worksheet >* **measure** *your* **rank** *on Google / Bing for sample keywords >* **restructure** *your website to better "talk to Google" vis-à-vis your keyword patterns.*

Let's look at some example websites.

Most businesses have a few different product or service lines, and often a few different customer segments. Take a look at Progressive Insurance (https://www.progressive.com/), for example, and you'll quickly realize that they have different types of insurance offered such as auto insurance, motorcycle insurance, RV insurance, and even Segway insurance. Take a look at https://www.progressive.com/insurance-choices/ to see the organizational structure of their website, and you'll quickly realize that the "structure" of the website reflects the "structure" of how people search for insurance. Those who are on a Harley-Davidson motorcycle are searching in one way, and those looking to ensure their Segway are searching in another.

So in terms of **keyword structural patterns** and **matching landing pages**, we have:

> *motorcycle insurance* = a group of keywords around *motorcycle insurance* like *cheap motorcycle insurance, motorcycle insurance quote,* etc. = a landing page on the website.

Car insurance = a group of keywords around *car insurance* like *cheap car insurance, automobile insurance, car insurance quote*, etc. = a landing page on the website.

etc.

Or, take a look at Industrial Fans Direct (http://www.industrialfansdirect.com/) and you'll see that they have product categories such as blowers, man coolers, ceiling, bathroom fans, etc., and that these reflect the "needs" of consumers who "search Google" using words that reflect those needs.

blowers = a group of keywords around *blowers* = a landing page on the website.

roof exhaust = a group of keywords around *roof exhaust* = a landing page on the website.

etc.

With those examples in mind, it's time to look at your own keyword patterns.

Take a look at your own **keyword brainstorm document**, and circle the "core keywords" that reflect your basic product or service categories. Usually you'll see a one-to-one correspondence of a "product group" that matches a "core keyword," as you see in the examples above. And you'll also see a bunch of helper words like *cheap, best, San Francisco, quote, rate*, etc., that are often entered alongside the core keyword. People often mistakenly think that they have "hundreds" of keywords, when in fact they usually have only about five to ten **core keyword groups** or **structural patterns**, and these then form hundreds of possible keyword queries. As on *Progressive.com* and *IndustrialFans.com* as listed above, you'll see that a core keyword should become one, and only one, landing page on the website.

Let me repeat that:

One *core keyword* will (ultimately) become one *landing page* on your website.

Looking at keywords for SEO in terms of core keywords makes it easy to see that a company will usually have about five to ten *core keywords*, and about five to ten corresponding *landing pages* on the website. (I'll explain landing pages in more detail in Chapters 3.1 and 3.2).

Keyword Volume and Value

As for keyword *volume* and *value*, you'll then see that you take a core keyword and you can look at the volume of the entire "group" of keywords around it, as well as the value as measured in Google's Keyword Planner that reflects the "value" of these keywords in the sense that they are likely, or not, to end in a sale.

Volume = are there a lot, or just a few, searches on Google that reflect the core keyword?

Value = if a searcher enters this search query is it of high, or low value, to your company, as measured in the likelihood that it can become a sale, and if it becomes a sale that that sale makes you a lot (or just a little) of money?

For your first **TODO**, download the **keyword worksheet**. For the worksheet, go to https://www.jm-seo.org/workbooks (click on 'SEO Fitness,' and enter the code '2017fitness' to register if you have not already done so), and click on the link to the "keyword worksheet." Note this is a Microsoft Excel document.

VIDEO. Watch a video tutorial on how to create a Keyword Worksheet at http://jmlinks.com/17m.

Inside the document, list each major pattern of your keywords (which reflect a product or service grouping of your company) on a line all by itself in the first column. Return to the Google AdWords Keyword Planner and note both the keyword volume and keyword value (suggested bid) that correspond to each core keyword.

➤ CREATE YOUR KEYWORD WORKSHEET

Now it's time to fill out your keyword worksheet in more detail. In your spreadsheet, you'll be filling out columns for the following:

> **Core Keywords**. These are the minimum words necessary to create a relevant search. If you are a watch repair shop servicing high-end watches, for example, your core keywords would be phrases such as "watch repair," "Tag Heuer Repair," "Rolex Repair," etc. This is the first column, and reflects the core, structural keyword patterns and indicates volume and value.
>
> > **Note.** If, to your business, a phrase is important enough (e.g., *Rolex watch repair* vs. *Tag Heuer watch repair* vs. just *watch repair*), then break it out into its own core keyword group / line item on your keyword worksheet. Do this even if these words are closely related (e.g., Rolex repair vs. Hamilton repair vs. Tag Heuer repair for watches).
>
> **Helper Keywords**. Common helpers are geographics like San Francisco, Berkeley, and Oakland. In the watch examples above, other helpers would be "best," "authorized," "NYC" etc. that combine with the core keywords to make the actual search query (e.g., "Best watch repair NYC").
>
> **Sample Search Query Phrases**. Take your core keywords plus your helpers and build out some "real" search queries that potential customers might use. Group these by keyword family. For example, you'd have a keyword group called "Rolex Repair" and underneath, related keyword phrases such as "Rolex Repair NYC," "Authorized Rolex Repair Midtown," or "Best Rolex Repair Shop New York," etc.
>
> **Search Volumes.** Indicate the volume of searches (where available) as obtained from the Google AdWords Keyword Planner.
>
> **Search Value.** Indicate whether a given keyword family is of high, low, or negative value to you and your business. Does it indicate a searcher who is probably a target customer? If your answer is strongly yes, then this is a "high value" search term! Does it clearly indicate a non-customer? If so, this is a "low value" or even a "negative" search term. I often mark "hot," "warm," or "cold" next to a keyword group.

Competitors. As you do your searches, write down the URL's of competitors that you see come up in your Google searches. These will be useful as mentors that you can emulate as you build out your SEO strategy.

Negative Keywords. Are there any keywords that indicate someone is definitely not your customer? Common examples are *cheap* or *free*, as these are often indicative of people with little or no money, or little or no intention to buy something. *(These negative keywords are not so important for SEO, but if you engage in AdWords, they will become very useful.)*

Priority Order

Not all keywords are created equally. Some are **high volume** (*lots of searches*), and some are **high value** (*they are customers ready to buy something, or take an important action like filling out a feedback form, or calling with an inquiry*). With respect to your business, take a look at your keyword worksheet and think about which queries are a) the *most likely* to be a potential sale, b) the *most likely* to be a high value sale, and c) the *least likely* to be ambiguous. (An ambiguous or problematic keyword is one that has several meanings, that might cross business products or services, and is, therefore, more difficult to optimize on than an unambiguous keyword. Compare *fan* for example, which could be a *hand fan*, an enthusiast for a *sports team*, or an *electrical appliance* to *blow air* with *insurance* which refers to one, and only one, type of product.)

VIDEO. Watch a video tutorial on educational vs. transactional, volume vs. value keyword theory at http://jmlinks.com/17n.

Prioritize Your Keywords: Hot, Warm, or Cold?

Prioritize your keyword families on the spreadsheet from TOP to BOTTOM with the highest priority keywords at the top, and the lowest at the bottom.

Remember the *volume* vs. *value* trade-off. "Transactional" keywords (those close to a sale) tend to have higher *value*, but lower *volume*; "whereas educational" keywords (those early in the research process) tend to have lower *value*, but higher *volume*.

However, here's the rub: because of the see-saw between value and volume, there is no hard and fast rule as to what should be your top priority. It can't be just *volume*, and it can't just be *value*.

In fact, I recommend you use a column on the far left and call it "hot / warm / cold." Sit down with the CEO or sales staff, and play a "hot / warm / cold" game by asking IF a customer entered such-and-such into Google, would it be hot (*definitely our customer*), warm (*probably our customer*), or cold (*not our customer*)?

Prioritize the "hot" keywords at the top of the Keyword Worksheet, and the "warm" keywords towards the bottom. I often throw out the "cold" keywords entirely. This will help you see the complexity of keyword patterns as some keywords will be "easy" to see as hot / warm / cold and others might be more challenging – perhaps they have a lot of volume, but are ambiguous, or perhaps they are high value but just so little volume, or the customers don't know to search for them.

> *The art of SEO is targeting the keywords most likely to generate high ROI, which is a function of BOTH volume and value.*

Competitive Level

Another tricky attribute is competition. As you research your keywords, pay attention to the competitive level. You can guess that a keyword is competitive (many vendors want to "get the click") based on:

- The **suggested bid** in the Keyword Planner: the *higher* the suggested bid, the *more competitive* a keyword.
- The **number of ads** shown for related search queries: the *more* ads you see, the *more competitive* a keyword.
- The *more* you see the **keyword phrase in the ads**: the *more* competitors have "discovered" a high-value keyword phrase, the more likely they are to include it in their ad headlines, and the *more competitive* is the keyword.

Remember, you can use the Keyword Planner to gauge the competitive level. Be sure to click on the *Columns Chevron* and enable "suggested bid" and "competition." Here's an example screenshot for *knee pain, knee surgery,* and *knee surgeon* for location of United States:

Note that *knee pain* has 110,000 average monthly searches, competitive level is "medium" and suggested bid is $3.69. Contrast that with *knee surgeon*, which has only 720 searches per month, but competition is seen as "high," and bid is at $4.96. *(Remember that this tool only gives you exact match: in those 720 searches are ONLY the exact phrase "knee surgeon." If the searcher typed in "best knee surgeons," that does not count in the total of twenty. Therefore, the tool grossly underestimates volume.)*

If you were a New York City knee surgeon building out his keyword worksheet, you'd want to prioritize "knee surgeon" and "knee surgery" over "knee pain," yet realize that the competitive level is higher for these terms.

> **VIDEO.** Watch a video tutorial about how to gauge competitive level at http://jmlinks.com/17q.

The Art of SEO

Don't stress your keyword organization too much!

Your keyword worksheet is a *living* document. As you build out your website, and measure your rank and results, you will "tune" your website to work on those keywords that are high value, high volume, and you can actually outcompete the competition for. It's a process, not a static result. SEO, like cooking great food or preparing for a marathon, is as much *art* as *science*. Don't fall prey to **analysis paralysis**, and endlessly analyze your keywords as opposed to implementing them.

Get a rough idea of your keywords, and then move on to implementation.

Search Patterns

For now, let's return to the structural patterns or keyword groups. It is very important to conceptualize the way that people search, i.e., the mindsets by which they approach your business. Let's take the example of Ron Gordon Watch Repair (https://www.rongordonwatches.com/). This business repairs luxury watches in New York City. What are the basic structural search patterns?

Watch Repair. These are searches built around the most basic search: "watch repair" and in some cases with the added helper geographic words of "NYC," "New York, NY" or "Manhattan." These are the more educational, less focused searches.

Watch Type Searches. These are searches by people who have a specific watch brand, e.g., Rolex, or Breitling. Their searches are much more focused such as "Breitling Repair NYC." Note that they are "specific" to a watch brand, and "specific" to a geography. And note that by the time they enter "Breitling Repair NYC" they are nearly ready to engage with a watch repair shop. These are the basic, transactional keyword patterns.

Micro or Long Tail Searches. These are searches by people who have a very specific watch need. It might be, "Rolex Battery Replacement NYC" or "Tissot Repair," which are searches that lack a lot of volume but are high value nonetheless. You're looking for micro or long tail searches that are transactional in nature.

Branded or Reputational Searches. Your brand image is very important to the success of your marketing. You want to monitor your online reputation by ranking highly for your branded or reputational searches, populating the Internet with positive information, and crowding out any negative information about your company. These are important for your keyword worksheet. A branded search, for example, is *Geico insurance* vs. a generic search such as *car insurance*. By the time someone is entering your company name as in *Geico insurance* they are close to a buy decision, and you want them to see flowers, sunshine, roses and positive information about your brand!

In sum, the **keyword worksheet** for your company should reflect keyword *volume*, *value* (as measured by the "fit" between the keyword search and what your company has to offer), and the *structural search patterns* that reflect the "mindset" by which people search.

VIDEO. Watch a quick video tutorial on building a keyword worksheet at http://jmlinks.com/17m.

≫ DELIVERABLE: YOUR KEYWORD WORKSHEET

After some brainstorming, hard work, and organization, you should have your first **DELIVERABLE** ready: a completed **keyword worksheet** in an Excel or Google spreadsheet. The first "dashboard" tab should be a high level overview to relevant keywords, reflecting the structural search patterns that generate the **keyword groups**, next the keyword volumes as measured by the Google keyword tool, and finally the values measured by the Google cost-per-click data and your own judgment as to which search queries are most likely to lead to a sale or sales lead. Other tabs (which you will fill out over time) include a tab for reporting, a tab to measure your rank on Google vs. keywords, a tab for local search rank, and a tab for landing pages.

Your keyword worksheet is your blueprint for successful SEO, but don't think of it as a static document! Rather, think of your keyword worksheet as an evolving "work in progress." There is as much art as science in SEO, and in many cases, the formal tools like the Keyword Planner only get you so far.

SEO and Cooking

Gut instinct as to how your customers search, especially which searches are likely to be close to a sale, is just as valuable as quantitative research! In fact, rather than think of SEO as a science, I strongly recommend you use other analogies. For example, I like to think of **SEO like cooking**: it has *technical elements* for sure, but it also has *inspiration* and a *je ne sais quoi* of tricks and techniques that you just have to "do" rather than "learn."

In fact, at my Stanford Continuing Studies class, I often have students watch a very fun video on Julia Child and then compare the art of SEO to the art of French cooking.

> **VIDEO.** Watch a quick video tutorial on how SEO is more like cooking than science at http://www.jmlinks.com/5q. Get motivated!

You cannot learn to cook by just reading cookbooks and philosophizing about cooking; you have to actually break some eggs, and make an omelet. And truly good cooks aren't just technical robots; they have a passion for their patrons, and an instinct about what makes something truly great. *SEO – like cooking – is an endeavor that has both technical and artistic elements.*

The point here is that although you should spend time researching the volume, value, and competitive levels of your target keywords, ultimately you'll see somewhere between five and ten keyword structural patterns. At that point it's "good enough" and you're ready to start optimizing your website. *Good cooks, cook, and good SEO's, do SEO.*

≫ MEASURE YOUR GOOGLE RANK VS. KEYWORDS

Now that you have built out your **keyword worksheet**, your next **TODO**, is to measure your **rank** on target Google searches. Google rank, of course, refers to whether your website is on the first page Google returns for a search queries. In the industry it's called *SERP rank* for "search engine results page rank." Counting the organic results only, there are positions 1, 2, and 3 (the "Olympic" positions) and then positions four through ten ("page one" positions). Anything beyond position ten is not good. *(Note that because of localization there is also your rank on the local "snack pack" of three local results originating in the Google+ system - more on this below.)*

You want to measure your website rank vis-à-vis your target keyword phrases, whether you are on page one (< 11) or in the "golden" positions of 1, 2, or 3.

Why Rank Matters

Why do we care about our Google rank? First of all, the Olympic positions (1, 2, and 3) capture the lion's share of clicks; by many estimates, over 60%! Second, being on page one (top ten results) means you are at least "in the game." But third, as good SEO experts, we want to measure our rank before, during and after our SEO efforts to measure our progress and return on investment (ROI). We can also feed this data back into our strategy so that we can then focus our content and link efforts (e.g. blog posts, product pages, press releases, link building) on searches where we are *beyond* page one vs. creating new content for searches for which we are *already* in top positions. Indeed, if you are spending money on Google AdWords advertising, you can use your rank for the organic results to optimize your spending; minimizing your spend on words for which you show "for free," and increasing your spend on keywords for which you do not rank well.

In short, measuring Google rank makes us work **smarter**, not **harder**!

Measure Your Rank Manually

You can measure your rank manually by simply entering your target search queries, and counting your position on the first page. Be sure to be "signed out" of your Google account or use "incognito mode" (http://jmlinks.com/18p) as Google customizes search results. You want to see your true rank on Google searches, not your personalized rank. Here are your steps:

1. Open up a web browser such as Google Chrome or Firefox in "incognito" or "private window" mode.
2. Go to Google.com.
3. Input a keyword phrase from your keyword worksheet.
4. Find your website, counting down from the top of the organic results.
   a. If you appear on page one, note your rank as in 1, 2, 3, 4, 5 up to 10. Be sure to count only the organic results, ignoring a) the ads on Google, and b) the local "snack pack" results which can be visible in a box of three on local searches such as "Sushi" or "probate lawyer," etc.
      i. If applicable, record the local "Snack Pack" rank separately as A (#1), B (#2) or C (#3).
   b. If you do NOT appear on page one, note your rank as NP (not present) as it doesn't really matter if you are position 11 or position 110 as few people go beyond page one.
5. Record your rank on your keyword worksheet, on the rank tab.
6. Repeat for other keywords on your keyword list.

Usually, a company will have between five and ten core keyword patterns, and between fifty and one hundred variations of keyword phrases built by combining the core keywords and helper words. Don't get discouraged if your rank is horrible when you begin an SEO project. Be positive: the only way you have to go is up!

Measure Your Rank Using Tools

While it's getting harder and harder to use free tools to measure your rank on Google because Google doesn't like to share this data with external companies, there remains one free tool that can systematically measure your rank: SEO Book's **Rank Checker for Firefox**. In addition, there are paid tools such as SERPS.com, AHrefs.com, and the MOZ.com tools that, for a fee, will measure your rank systematically. This makes it much easier to track your rank on Google, Bing, or Yahoo vs. keyword targets on a daily, weekly, or monthly basis. I highly recommend signing up for the Moz.com toolsuite, as it's the cheapest yet most robust set of tools out there with pricing of around $99 a month. Check my *SEO Toolbook* or Dashboard at http://jmlinks.com/seodash for a complete list of rank checking tools, both free and paid.

How to Use Rank Checker

Here are instructions on how to use Rank Checker.

Go to http://www.seobook.com/ and sign up for a free account. Next, find the Rank Checker tool on the pull down menus; and download the tool. Remember: it is available only for Firefox, so if you don't have Firefox, you'll first need to download it for free at http://www.firefox.com/.

Once the tool is downloaded and installed as a Firefox plugin, enter your keyword list in the tool as follows. In the file menu, select Tool > Rank Checker > Run. Then click "Add Multiple" keywords. Enter your target keywords plus your domain. In the "Options" tab (Tool, Rank Checker, and Options), be sure to check "Don't use Google Personalized Results" and set "Delay between Queries" to 5 seconds to analyze ten words or less; to 99 seconds if you are going to run a very long list.

(The reason is Google will stop giving you data if you poll it too rapidly).

Here's a screenshot showing how to get to the Rank Checker tool via the Firefox menu:

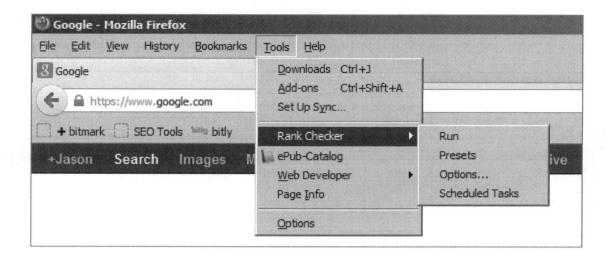

Once you're inputted your keyword list, and run your first report, you can export the data into CSV / Excel format by choosing "export" at the lower left hand part of the screen.

Record Your Keyword Rank Data

I recommend recording your keyword rank on at least a monthly basis, and inputting this into your keyword worksheet on the rank tab. This will give you a baseline before, during, and after you start your SEO project.

On an on-going basis, use the resulting rank data to identify "strengths" (places where you appear in the top three or top ten) and "weaknesses" (keywords for which you appear beyond page one, or not at all). Having identified your keyword rank weaknesses, you now know where to target your SEO efforts!

> **VIDEO.** Watch a quick video tutorial on measuring keyword rank at http://www.jmlinks.com/50.

Another good free tool to check your rank on Google is the FAT Rank Chrome Plugin at http://jmlinks.com/18q. Available for Chrome (not Firefox), you simply install the plugin. Next, visit your website home page, and then click the Pokemon-looking icon in the top right of your Chrome browser. Enter the keyword phrase that you want to check your Google rank for. Here's a screenshot:

Remember: you MUST first visit your own website, and NEXT click on the FATRANK icon to enable this tool. Then, you enter your keyword.

VIDEO. Watch a video on how to measure your rank using FAT Rank as well as the Google AdWords Preview tool at http://jmlinks.com/18h.

Paid Rank-checking Tools

If you have money for a **paid rank-checking tools**, I recommend Serps.com, Ahrefs.com, or the Moz tools at moz.com. The reality is that Google does not like people to systematically track their rank on Google searches, so paying one of these vendors a monthly fee for their tool will make your life much, much easier than using a free rank-checking tool.

Measure Local Search Results Manually

As you check rank, be sensitive to the fact that the free tools generally measure only your organic rank on a non-localized basis. Google "localizes" search results, especially short tail phrases: searchers in different cities, see different results. For example, a search for "probate attorney" in Dallas will return Dallas probate attorneys, whereas the same search in San Francisco will return San Francisco probate attorneys. This happens with many "short tail" searches that have a local character such as: *attorney, CPA, accountant, pizza, sushi, massage therapist, marriage counselor*, etc. – any search terms that generally indicate someone is looking for a local small business.

The free Rank Checker tools listed above, unfortunately, do **NOT** calculate your rank in a localized fashion. Therefore, if **local search rankings** are important to you, you need to **manually** check your rank on Google+ local as shown in the "snack pack" usually consisting of three results on Google.

To check your local rank (varying your position city-by-city), use the Google AdWords Preview Tool at http://jmlinks.com/18r or the free SERPS local rank checking tool at http://jmlinks.com/18s.

> **VIDEO.** Watch a video on how to measure your local rank using the Google AdWords Preview tool at http://jmlinks.com/17s.

Here's a screenshot showing the search for "Pizza" and the "snack pack" of three local results with location of Fremont, California:

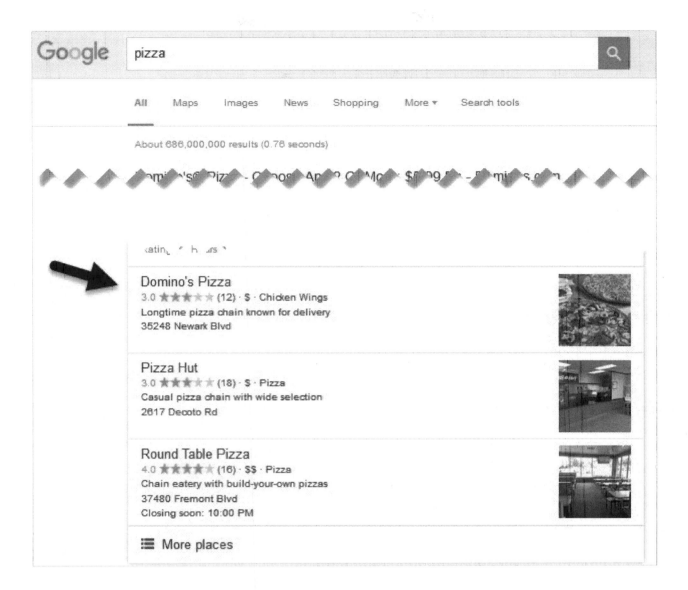

In this example, therefore, you'd record position #1 (A) for Domino's, #2 (B) for Pizza Hut, and #3 (C) for Round Table Pizza. Positions greater than #3 appear on the "second page" of local results (on both the phone and the desktop) and are worth considerably less than positions, #1, #2, and #3. (Note: it has become industry-standard practice to record local rank in the "snack pack" as A / B / C not 1 / 2 / 3).

For your own company, identify short tail local searches and record these on your keyword worksheet, on the "local rank" tab.

Measuring Your Rank in Different Cities

Let's say you want to look at your locations in multiple cities such as San Francisco, San Jose, and Oakland. You cannot do this directly in Google, you have to use the AdWords preview tool which you can get to directly in AdWords by logging in, and on the top menu, selecting Tools > Preview Tool. Alternatively, you can access the preview tool directly at this URL http://jmlinks.com/13m.

Here's a screenshot of the tool with location set to Tulsa, Oklahoma, and search term set to *accountants*:

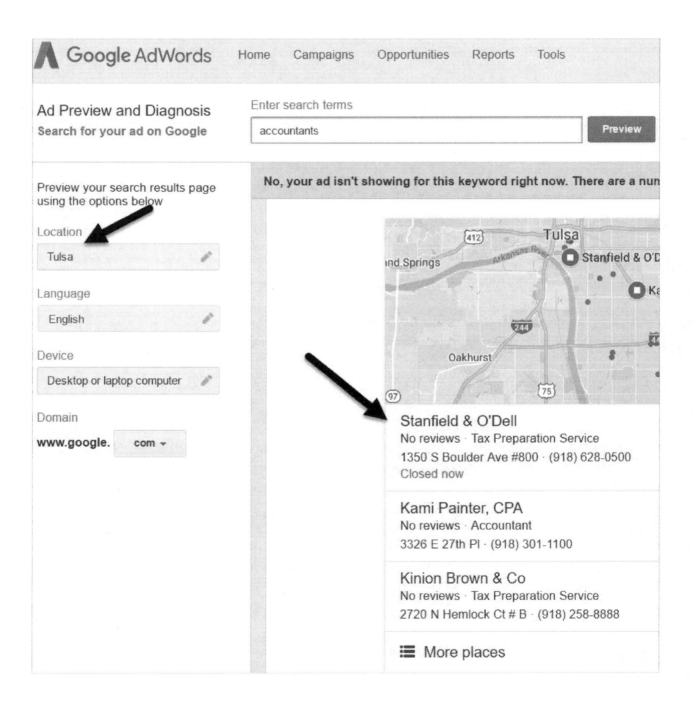

(You can ignore that "No, your ad isn't showing" blurb as that refers to advertising).

If you want to measure your local rank, you'll need to manually change the tool city by city. In addition to the "snack pack," notice that the organic ranks themselves will also change for localized keywords. So, in this case, you'll have to manually rank check both your rank in the snack pack and in the organic results.

Finally, you can also vary the view as desktop, tablet, or mobile phone, and in this way also measure your rank on various devices. To do this, change the "Device" on the far left column. Mobile rank does not yet vary as dramatically as rank based on localization but it does vary.

> **VIDEO.** Watch a quick video tutorial on using Google and/or the AdWords Preview Tool to measure your local rank at http://jmlinks.com/17s.

Because of localization and differences on rank for mobile, tablet, and desktop, it can be very time-consuming to measure your rank for fifty to a hundred keywords and many tens of target cities! For this reason, if local SEO matters a lot to you, I highly recommend paying for a *paid* rank-checking tool such as Serps.com, as this tool can measure your rank in different cities for many different keywords in a systematic and automated fashion. Time is money, and a paid rank-checking tool will save you a lot of time!

»» DELIVERABLE: RANK MEASUREMENT AND A BASELINE SCORE

The final **DELIVERABLE** for this Chapter is to measure your rank across a statistical sample of between twenty and one hundred keywords, depending on how complex your company is. Using either free or paid tools, input these data on a monthly basis into your keyword worksheet rank tab(s).

3.1

PAGE TAGS

Once you know your keywords via **Step #2**, where do you put them? "Page Tag" SEO is the quick and easy answer to that question, and it is the most important aspect of **Step #3**. In **Step #3**, you take your keywords from your keyword worksheet, place them in strategic locations on individual web pages via **page tags**, **restructure** your website to send clear signals to Google about your keyword targets, and finally conduct a **website audit** to identify necessary tag and structural changes.

Let's get started!

TODO LIST:

» Understand Page Tags, HTML, and Talking to Google

» Page Tags and Poker

» Weave Keywords into Page Tags

» A Visual Test for Keyword Density

»» Deliverable: A Completed Page Tag Worksheet

» Set Up Your Home Page

»» Deliverable: A Completed Home Page Page Tag Worksheet

» UNDERSTAND PAGE TAGS, HTML, AND TALKING TO GOOGLE

HTML is the language of the Web, and it is based on what are called "tags" in HTML. At a very simple level, if you want a word to appear bold on a web page, you put the "tag" **<strong>** around the word such as *"We sell **<strong>**running shoes**</strong>**"* in the HTML text of the web page. This will display in browsers as:

We sell **running shoes**.

If you are using a WYSIWYG editor like WordPress or Dreamweaver, the editor will "hide" this code from you, but behind the scenes the true foundation of the Web is HTML, and the foundation of HTML is **page tags**. For a super simple introduction to HTML, visit http://jmlinks.com/13n.

HTML: the Browser, the Website, & Google

Here's what most people do, and don't, understand about page tags and the Web:

- **The Browser.** Page Tags such as <strong>, <a href>, <img alt>, etc., structure how the browser displays information to the user – bold, a link, an image, etc. (*This, they understand*).
- **The Website.** Page Tags structure the interrelationship between pages on a website, especially through <a href>, the "anchor" or "link" tag but also through CSS style sheets. (*This, they understand*).
- **Google and other Search Engines**. Page Tags send signals to Google about what keywords are important with respect to an individual website, and even the website as a whole (*This, few people understand*).

Viewing the HTML Source / Page Tags

To see the true HTML behind the visible Web, go to any webpage with your browser, right click on your mouse, select "View Source" in Firefox, Internet Explorer, or Chrome. (Note: the keyboard shortcut to view source code is CTRL+U (PC) or Command+U (Mac)). The HTML code you see is the true language of the Web, and this code is what Google or Bing actually uses to index a web page. For example, here is a screenshot of the HTML source code for Geico's page on "Motorcycle Insurance" (https://www.geico.com/motorcycle-insurance/) with the word motorcycle highlighted in yellow:

Here's their TITLE tag:

```
<title>Motorcycle        Insurance      Quotes      Online      |
GEICO</title>
```

The TITLE tag controls the top of the browser, the text you see if you bookmark this page, and the headline of the page on Google. And here's their H1 (Header) tag:

```
<h1>Start     a     free     motorcycle     insurance     <span
class="line-break">quote          to          see          the
savings.</span></h1>
```

The H1 makes this sentence appear in a big bold font.

Most people understand that this HTML code structures how the browser displays the information about Geico's landing page on *motorcycle insurance.* But what they miss is that this HTML code is also sending **powerful signals to Google about keyword targets**.

In a very simple way, if your page has ****running shoes**** on it, you are not just bolding the word *running shoes* in the browser; you are also signaling Google that the keyword phrase *running shoes* is important to you!

PAGE TAGS SIGNAL KEYWORD PRIORITIES TO GOOGLE

If, for example, you write an HTML page like this:

```
<h1>Learn about our Car Insurance</h1>
We sell the best <strong>car insurance</strong> in Houston
```

Which will render in a browser like Chrome, Firefox, or Safari as:

Learn About Car Insurance

We sell the best **car insurance** in Houston

This is doing two things:

1. Telling the **Web browser** to render the first sentence in big, bold letters, and to render the phrase car insurance in bold text.
2. **Signaling** to **Google** that the words: *Learn, About, Car, Insurance* are important to you – these are words that you would like to rank for on Google. (Google ignores common words like learn or about, which are called "stop words" and instead will see *car* and *insurance* as the important words).

Similarly, by placing the words *motorcycle insurance* into strategic tags such as the TITLE and H1 tags, Geico is signaling Google that this page is about *motorcycle insurance* and not about *RV insurance* or *dog toys*. It's a clear and unambiguous communication to Google about the keyword target.

Your Website is Your Google Resume

Remember the "Job Search" analogy? Your *website* is like a *resume*. If you are looking for a job as a ***BMW auto mechanic***, then you would BOLD the words ***auto***, ***mechanic***, and ***BMW*** on your resume, wouldn't you? That bolding would not only make the words appear blacker on the page, it would also "signal" to the person reading your resume that you want to "rank" (i.e., be considered for a job for) those terms.

Your Website = a Resume

Manipulating Page Tags = Bolding / Making Bigger Keywords on the Resume = signals to Google

The concept in terms of SEO is to realize that the tag structure of a web page does two things:

1. Talk to "humans" by making some text **BIG**, and some text *italics*, some text a **HEADLINE** and other text just text, some images ON THE PAGE, and some cross-links so humans can click from one page to another.
2. Talk to "Google," by using the same tags to communicate which keywords are IMPORTANT and which keywords are not very important.

Now that I've drilled this concept into your head through repetition (*it's that important*!), you should realize that you must design for two audiences: humans and Google.

DESIGN YOUR WEBSITE

FOR HUMANS AND GOOGLE

Fortunately, you do not have to be an HTML expert. You need to understand just the basics of HTML because modern WYSIWYG editors like WordPress do the HTML coding for you. Using WordPress, for example, here's a screenshot of my webpage on *AdWords Expert Witness* services as seen inside of WordPress:

I have highlighted the Page Title (which becomes the TITLE tag), and the H2 (which becomes the Header 2 Tag) in yellow. The red arrows show where you can change the header tag in WordPress, as well as where the actual header text is located. You can view the actual page on the Web at http://jmlinks.com/5r. (Right click, and view source to see the HTML code that underlies the browser-visible web page).

In this way, WordPress makes it easy to "speak HTML" and "talk to Google." You just have to know which tags are important for SEO, and how to get those tags implemented in WordPress. (If you are using another editor, such as Squarespace or Dreamweaver, accordingly, you have to figure out what items in the editor yield what items in HTML).

Finally, if you are using WordPress, I highly recommend the Yoast WordPress Plugin at http://jmlinks.com/5s. It enables you to "split" the WordPress TITLE from the SEO-friendly TITLE tag, as well as easily add a META DESCRIPTION tag to your pages.

By inserting keywords into your HTML Page Tags, you are "talking to Google." You want, however, to do more than talk to Google: you want to win.

But which tags send the strongest signals?

To understand which tags are the most important, let's use a new analogy: **page tags are like the cards in poker**.

PAGE TAGS =

POKER CARDS

Now any good poker player knows that the *Ace* is more powerful than the *King*, and the *King* more powerful than the *Deuce*, and that *Full House* beats *two of a kind*. These are the "rules of poker."

Now, could you go to Las Vegas and attempt poker without knowing which cards have which values? Of course you could! The "house" and the other players at the table would love to take all your money. They love it when you sluff away your Aces and keep your deuces!

But you'll do much better if you learn the card values, and some basic strategies.

Similarly, once you realize that Page Tags are like poker cards, you'll quickly realize that you can build a website without understanding which cards communicate what to Google. (And your website wouldn't perform well in terms of SEO, and it would be like most of the terrible, no good, rotten, horrible, mal-adjusted SEO websites on the Internet).

It gets worse.

Now, could you build a website without understanding HTML Page Tag values for SEO? Of course you could: the "house" (a.k.a. Google) and the other players would love to take all your money. *Google will be happy to take your money by forcing you to pay to advertise via AdWords, and your competitors are happy to take your money by forcing you off the first page of Google.*

The poker table, my friend, is cruel.

However, once you realize that HTML tags are like Poker cards... your next step is to learn their values.

Let's play poker with Google!

To begin, examine the following table showing the most important page tags "as if" you were playing a game of poker with Google and your competitors:

TAG	POKER	COMMENT
<TITLE>	Ace	Most important tag on any page, place your target keyword in the <TITLE> tag of each page. <TITLE> of the home page is the most powerful tag on any website. (59 visible characters; 80 indexed).
<A HREF>	King	Keyword-heavy links cross reference pages to each other, and communicate keywords to Google.
<IMG ALT>	Queen	Have at least one image per page, and put your target keyword into the ALT attribute of the image.
<H1>	Jack	Google loves the header family, so use at least one <H1> per page. Use <H2>, <H3> sparingly.
<META DESCRIPTION >	10	If you include the target keyword in the <META DESCRIPTION> tag, Google will use it 90% of the time. (155 character limit).
<BODY> or keyword density	9	Write keyword-heavy prose on each and every page of the website. Aim for natural syntax and about 5% keyword density.
<STRONG>, <B>, <EM>	3, 4, 5	Use bold and italicize keywords on the page, strategically.
<META KEYWORDS>	Joker	Ignored by Google. Use it as a "note to self" about the keyword targets for a particular page.

The above table is very important. It tells you that once you know the target keyword for a given page, then place that keyword inside of the <TITLE>, <A HREF>, <IMG ALT>, <H1>, <META DESCRIPTION> and <BODY> (visible content). Don't overdo this, but don't underdo it, either. (*More on writing Google-friendly content in a moment*)

Get and Read Google's Official SEO Starter Guide

Google produces a very good official guide to SEO that emphasizes just how important tag structure is to Google and SEO. I strongly recommend that you download the guide and read it thoroughly at http://jmlinks.com/googleseo. It doesn't tell you everything, but it's a good, basic guide to On Page SEO, the art and science of structuring your content to "talk" to Google in terms of your target keywords.

Besides explaining the basics of On Page SEO, the guide also has two other usages:

Sleep Aid. It is an excellent sleep aid, so when you just can't get drowsy, simply start reading. You'll be dreaming ZZZZZs in no time. (*I keep a copy under my pillow for this very reason*).

Attack Weapon. If you're working with a recalcitrant web designer, team member, or CEO, who doesn't believe what I'm telling you in this book because I'm "just" *Jason McDonald SEO guru of San Francisco, California*, print out the guide on paper. Next, you can roll up the guide, and start beating him or her on the head, explaining: HERE'S A CRAZY IDEA. TO GET TO THE TOP OF GOOGLE CAN WE PLEASE JUST DO WHAT GOOGLE TELLS US TO DO? If you print the guide with an inkjet and moisten it prior to the beating, you may also be able to get the Google logo to bleed off onto their forehead.

Seriously, the guide is a great basic, official guide to On Page SEO and should be required reading for anyone on your team involved in search engine optimization.

Hate reading? Here are some videos:

VIDEO. Watch a video tutorial of TITLE, META DESCRIPTION and KEYWORDS "meta" tags for SEO at http://jmlinks.com/17r as well as a video on how to do a page tag analysis at http://jmlinks.com/5u.

I also highly recommend you read my "SEO Page Tag Template" at http://jmlinks.com/18t. The end result of page tags is to understand that page tags communicate your keywords to Google, so your first **TODO** is pretty obvious: weave your keywords into your page tags, starting with the all-important TITLE tag.

Basically:

Target keyword > embed in TITLE, META DESCRIPTION, HEADER, IMG ALT and VISIBLE PAGE CONTENT

Now, do NOT overdo this! *"A little salt is good for the soup, but too much salt ruins the soup."* You want to take a specific landing page, and focus Google's attention around one, and only one, keyword phrase.

Audit High-Ranking Pages and "Reverse Engineer" Their Page Tags

Now that you know how Page Tags "talk" to Google, revisit some top-ranking pages especially by companies like Geico, Progressive, or eSurance that clearly practice high-stakes SEO. Revisit Google searches like "motorcycle insurance," "car insurance," or even "Segway insurance," and see how the winning websites are "speaking Google" vis Page Tags.

The insurance industry is an excellent place to look for SEO Olympians!

For example, revisit a high-ranking page such as the page on Progressive.com for "Segway Insurance" (https://www.progressive.com/segway/) view the source code via CTRL+U / COMMAND+U, do a CTRL+F / COMMAND+F and search for "Segway Insurance," and notice how that target keyword phrase ("Segway Insurance") has been strategically embedded into the tag structure and visible content. Compare it with other top-ranking pages such as https://www.esurance.com/insurance/segway and notice how they do the same. These pages are using Page Tags to communicate to Google that they want to rank for "Segway Insurance."

VIDEO. Watch a quick video tutorial of a page autopsy at http://jmlinks.com/5v.

Now, toggle back to your sad, pathetic web pages, and notice how inefficiently they are talking to Google. (*I'm joking – I want you to stay positive*! They're not sad and pathetic, they're "ready to work" and "ready for you to optimize them"). Now, toggle back to your web pages and have your "Aha" moment and realize that you need to revise their keywords / page content vis-à-vis their page tag structure to "speak Google."

≫ WEAVE KEYWORDS INTO PAGE TAGS

In summary, now that you know that the TITLE tag is the most important tag, that Google likes the header tag family, that each web page should have at least one image tag with the ALT attribute defined to include a keyword, and should link across to other web pages based on your target keywords, you are ready to write a strong SEO page or re-write an existing page to better communicate keyword priorities to Google.

Page Tags and Keywords for All Pages Except the Home Page

We will deal with the home page separately, because the home page is incredibly important to SEO and has unique responsibilities. But, for all pages EXCEPT the home page, here's how to write SEO-friendly content for one, and only one, specific page:

1. **Define your target keywords**. Using your keyword worksheet as well as the various keyword tools, define the target keywords for the specific page. A best practice is to focus on a single keyword per individual landing page or blog post.
2. **Write a keyword-heavy TITLE tag**. The TITLE tag should be less than 80 characters, with the most important keywords on the left. The first 59 characters will generally appear on Google as your headline.
3. **Write a keyword-heavy META DESCRIPTION tag**. The META DESCRIPTION tag has a 90% chance of being the visible description on Google, so write one that includes your keywords but is also pithy and exciting. Its job is to "get the click" from Google. Character limit is 155 characters.
4. **Write a few keyword-heavy header tags**. Start with an H1 tag and throw in a couple of H2 tags around keyword phrases.
5. **Include at least one image with the ALT attribute defined**. Google likes to see at least one image on a page, with the keywords around the ALT attribute.
6. **Cross-link via keyword phrases**. Embed your target keyword phrases in links that link your most important pages across your website to each other around keyword phrases.
7. **Write keyword dense text**. Beyond just page tags, Google looks to see a good keyword density (about 3-5%) and keywords used in natural English syntax following good grammar.

Presto! You now "speak Google."

Don't

Overdo it!

Finally, don't *overdo* it! That's called *keyword stuffing* and it's dangerous.

▶ A Visual Test for SEO-friendly Keyword Density

As you are writing new pages or analyzing existing ones, keep in mind that **keyword density** on the Web is much, much more **redundant** than in normal English writing.

Few SEO experts and even fewer average marketers really realize just how *redundant, repetitious, repeating, reinforcing,* and *reiterating* strong prose is for Google! Furthermore, it's not just about stringing keywords in comma, comma, and comma phrases. The Google algorithm, post-Panda, clearly analyzes text and looks for natural syntax, so be sure to write in complete sentences following the rules of grammar and spelling.

So, write keyword heavy text in natural English syntax sentence, while avoiding comma, comma, and comma phrases. What keyword density is "just right?"

Here's a screenshot of the Geico motorcycle insurance page, using CTRL+F in Firefox to highlight the occurrences of the word "motorcycle":

Let's Ride® – Get Your Motor Running and Get a Motorcycle Insurance Quote.

Rev up your savings with motorcycle insurance from GEICO. No matter what you own – a sport bike, cruiser, standard, touring bike, or a sweet custom ride, you can turn to us for great rates and great coverage. We even offer scooter insurance. Enjoy the freedom of the open road knowing that the Gecko®'s got your back! Let's Ride®

Get free motorcycle insurance quotes anytime.

Why Choose GEICO for Motorcycle Insurance?

Thought that GEICO was all about car insurance, did you? Think again! We take motorcycles as seriously as you do, and we're pleased to provide you with top-quality coverage for your bike. With GEICO, you get:

> Outstanding customer service (rated 4.7 out of 5 by our motorcycle insurance

How keyword dense is a page? I call this the "pink and pinch test". Find pages for very competitive Google searches (such as "motorcycle insurance" or "reverse mortgage" or "online coupons"), highlight their keywords by using CTRL+F in Firefox, read the text aloud and pinch yourself every time the keyword is used. At the end of the page, you should be in pain! If you are not in pain, the density is too low. If you're in the hospital, it's too high. In terms of metrics, a good rule of thumb is 3-5 % density, but remember also that it's not just numeric density but the occurrence of keywords in normal sentences that matter.

EYE CANDY AT TOP

TEXT AT BOTTOM

Page Content: What Comes First?

Google likes text, but people like pictures. There is a trade-off between the heavy, redundant text favored by Google and the clean, iPhone like picture websites favored by humans. The usual solution is to put the eye candy for humans towards the *top*, and the stuff for Google towards the *bottom*. Revisit many of the pages on Geico.com or Progressive.com and you'll notice how the eye candy for humans is at the top, and the redundant text for Google is at the bottom.

A page that does this in a really obvious way is http://www.sfflowershop.com/ (scroll to the bottom, and be horrified).

It ranks well on Google for searches like *same day flower delivery San Francisco*, and it sells flowers – what's there to complain about?

The Panda Update

Periodically Google updates its algorithm, to improve the search results and combat what is called "Web spam." One of the most important algorithm updates was called **Panda**, and Panda specifically targeted *keyword stuffing*, which is the overuse of keywords on a page. In this post-Panda world, the key thing to do is to hit a "sweet spot" of just enough keyword density but not so much as to trigger a penalty. Even more important, don't think of **keyword density** as a simple numeric percentage, but rather as the strategic weaving of keywords into HTML tags and text. Here are post-Panda principles to writing SEO-friendly content:

1. **Know your keywords**. Keywords remain as important as ever! In addition to your focus keyword, however, look for **related** or **adjacent** keywords. A page targeting "motorcycle insurance" for example should have sentences that also contain words like *riding, rate, quote, Harley-Davidson*, etc. Use Google Autocomplete and Google related searches functions to find "adjacent" words and weave them into your content.
2. Use **natural syntax** and **good grammar**. Write like educated people talk, and write using good *subject, verb, object* structure. Gone are the days when you could just write *keyword, keyword, keyword*. I recommend you should read your page content out loud: it should sound heavier than normal English in terms of keywords, but not so heavy as you sound crazy. Grammar- and spell-check your final visible content.
3. **Avoid comma, comma, comma phrases**; another way of saying write normal, natural prose (but still containing your keywords!). Google is aware of

the obvious tricks such as sentences with twenty-five commas, and white text on a white background. Don't be stupid.

4. **Don't be too perfect**. Don't have an optimized, perfect TITLE and META DESCRIPTION and ALT ATTRIBUTE for an IMAGE, etc. – mix things up a bit.

Post-Panda, the trick is to be keyword heavier than normal English, but still retain good, natural syntax. *A little salt is good in the soup; too much salt ruins it.*

A good litmus test is:

- Does your page contain the target keywords in the key HTML tags yet with some variety and adjacent keywords? And,
- If a "normal" person reads your page, will he or she be unaware that it has been optimized for SEO yet hear the keyword phrase loud and clear? And,
- Does the page actually convey useful information to the human reader?

If the answer is YES to these questions, you'll probably survive Panda. If the answer is NO, you are either underoptimized (*keywords do not appear in key tags*) or overoptimized (*text is clunky and weird to "normal" humans*).

Another easy rule-of-thumb. Do your target searches and look at the content of the current "winners." Find the middle ground characterized by the winners in your industry and be as text heavy and dense as they are, but not aggressively more so.

Keywords No Longer Matter?

Finally, you may read on the blogosphere that "keywords no longer matter." This is an incredibly stupid and dangerous idea, based largely on ignorance and on Google propaganda about so-called semantic search. "Just write for humans and don't worry about SEO, or SEO-friendly page tags," is a common refrain among the ignorant.

Why do keywords still matter? Here's why.

First, people type keywords into Google and speak keywords into their mobile phones and these words are the "connection points" indicating what they want Google to go out an "find" for them. Secondly, language in and of itself is *sui generis* based on keywords, and Google isn't going to change language. We don't beat around the bush, we say things like, "Honey do you want **PIZZA** tonight?" to our wives and "Excuse me, do you know where the **TOILET PAPER,**" is to the employees at the supermarket. So keywords mark what we want in actual human language. They are not going away! Third, the *keywords META tag* is ignored but this confusion between a META tag and keywords causes even more confusion. It's the META tag that's ignored, not keywords. And, finally, this idea that "keywords don't matter" is based on a false choice: either you write FOR PEOPLE or you write FOR GOOGLE, when in fact, you can write for both.

> *Aim for the sweet spot of keyword density high enough for Google but not so high as to be unreadable, or "stuffed" in the parlance of SEO. A little salt is good for the soup, and too much salt ruins it. But you need salt to make soup!*

To use another analogy: as I always tell my wife on our yearly road trips: speed a little, honey, but don't be the fastest car on the Interstate. If you don't speed, you won't get there first (or near first), but if you drive the red car, right past the cop at 120 mph, you'll get pulled over. Don't underdo your keyword density, and don't overdo it either (welcome to post-*Panda* SEO content).

Oh, and don't believe everything you read on the blogosphere. A lot of it is pure dribble.

» DELIVERABLE: A COMPLETED PAGE TAG WORKSHEET (FOR ONE PAGE)

The first **DELIVERABLE** for Step Three is a completed **page tag worksheet** for one specific landing page, other than your home page. Take either a new page or an existing page of your website, and compare it against the desired target keyword. (Note: each page should have one, and only one, keyword target. Using the "page tag worksheet," audit the page for how well it communicates the keyword target to Google. For the worksheet, go to https://www.jm-seo.org/workbooks (click on "SEO Fitness 2017," and enter the code '2017fitness' to register if you have not already done so), and click on the link to the "page tag worksheet." Note: you'll want to do this at least for all of your major landing pages.

A nifty tool to use to help you audit existing pages can be found at http://jmlinks.com/5w. (If your pages are in the *https://* format you can use http://jmlinks.com/13p).

Input your own web page into the tool and check it. The page's target keywords should be clearly and prominently indicated in the tool; if not, you are not correctly signaling keyword priorities to Google. For more nifty tools to help with Page Tags, refer to my SEO dashboard at https://www.jm-seo.org/dashboard/seo and scroll down to the subsection called Page Tags.

>> SET UP YOUR HOME PAGE

Page tag SEO applies to your home page, but your home page is so important you should handle it in a very specific way. Your home page is your "front door" to Google and the **most important page** of your website. Google rewards beefy, keyword-heavy home pages that have a lot of text. Think carefully about every word that occurs on this page, and about the way each word is "structured" by embedding it into good HTML page tags. Here are your important "to do's" for your home page:

- ✓ **Identify your customer-centric, top three keywords.** These three "most important" words must go into your home page <TITLE> tag, the most powerful tag on your website!
- ✓ **Repeat the <TITLE> tag content in the <H1> tag on the page.** There should be at least one <H1> but no more than three per page.
- ✓ **Identify your company's major product / service offerings.** Re-write these using customer centric keywords, and have <H2> tags leading to these major landing pages, nested inside of <A HREF> tags. Be sure to include the keywords inside the <H2> and <A HREF> tags!
- ✓ **Have Supporting Images.** Google rewards pages that have images with ALT attributes that are keyword heavy. Don't overdo this, but have at least one and no more than about seven images on your home page that have keywords in their ALT attributes.
- ✓ **Create keyword-focused one click links**. Link down from your home page to defined landing pages around target keyword phrases.
- ✓ **Write lengthy, keyword-rich content for your home page.** You need not just structural elements, but lots of beefy prose on your home page that clarifies to Google what your company is "about."

For good home page ideas, look at Progressive (https://www.progressive.com/) or eSurance (https://www.esurance.com/), as well as some of SEO-savvy Bay Area medical malpractice attorneys such as http://www.danroselaw.com/ or http://www.bayareamedicalmalpractice.com/. If you're into flowers, check out http://www.sfflowershop.com/. Scroll to the bottom and notice all the keyword heavy text "buried" for Google to find! View their HTML source and look at how they weave their keywords into strategic tags. Now, some of this is clearly overdone, but the point is to see that effective SEO home pages have a lot of text, contain the target keywords, and embed the keywords in key tags often with links "down" to specific landing pages.

> **VIDEO.** Watch a quick video tutorial on effective SEO home pages at http://jmlinks.com/18g.

Or, choose your own industry, do some high level searches on Google or Bing, and reverse engineer the home pages of the winners at SEO. Then, proceed to audit your own home page: how effectively does your own home page "speak Google?"

In auditing your home page, it should:

- Have a **TITLE tag** that succinctly explains your business value proposition, and includes at least three highly valued keywords in the first 59 characters.
- Have a **META description** tag that explains your business value proposition, contains your keywords, and is written in a pithy, exciting way to "get the click" from Google to your website. The character limit, of course, is 155 characters.
- Follow the **principles of Page Tag SEO** by weaving your keywords into the main tags such as the H1 / H2 family, the A HREF anchor tag, the IMG alt tags, etc.
- Have **keyword-dense, well-written text** that explains what you do and contains your target keywords.
- Have "**one click**" links down to your most important landing pages.

It should also be visually appealing to humans, and lead to a desired action such as a sale or a registration form. Don't forget the carbon-based life forms!

≫ DELIVERABLE: A HOME PAGE PAGE TAG AUDIT

In the next chapter, we'll learn a bit more about how website structure influences Google and SEO, but we can begin the process now by doing a page tag audit for your home page. The most powerful tag on your website is the home page TITLE tag, so start there.

Drill down to the text content on your home page and verify that it contains the priority keyword targets identified in your keyword worksheet.

> **WORKSHEETS.** For your **DELIVERABLE**, analyze your home page's existing Page Tag vs. target keyword status, and devise a "quick fix" strategy to improve keyword placement in important tags. For the worksheet, go to https://www.jm-seo.org/workbooks (click on "SEO Fitness 2017," enter the code '2017fitness' to register if you have not already done so), and click on the link to the "home page worksheet."

SURVEY OFFER

CLAIM YOUR $10 REBATE OR FREE BOOK! HERE'S HOW –

7. Visit http://jmlinks.com/survey.
8. Take a short, simple survey about the book.
9. Indicate whether you want a $10.00 rebate or a free copy of one of Jason's other books on SEO / Social Media Marketing / Job Search & Career-building.

WE WILL THEN –

- Rebate you the $10.00, or send you a free copy of one of the other books.

~ $10 REBATE OFFER ~

~ LIMITED TO ONE PER CUSTOMER ~

EXPIRES: 3/1/2017

SUBJECT TO CHANGE WITHOUT NOTICE

GOT QUESTIONS? CALL 800-298-4065

3.2

WEBSITE STRUCTURE

Website structure - the "organization" of your website - is a major part of **Step #3**. Whereas in **page tags** you approach SEO from the perspective of individual web pages, in website structure you should turn your attention to how your *entire* website communicates keyword priorities to Google. How you name your files, how you "reach out" to Google, and how you optimize your landing pages all combine to make a *good* SEO strategy, *great*!

Let's get started!

TODO LIST:

>> Define SEO Landing Pages

>> >> Deliverable: Landing Page List

>> Write a Keyword Heavy Footer

>> Create a Blog and Start Blogging

>> Use Keyword Heavy URLs over Parameter URLs

>> Leverage the Home Page for One Click Links

>> Join Google and Bing Webmaster Tools

>> >> Deliverable: Website Structure Worksheet

>> DEFINE SEO LANDING PAGES

In SEO, a **landing page** is a page you create that targets very **specific keyword phrases**. For most companies, your landing pages will reflect your product or service offerings, adjusted for how "real customers" search for them on Google. Companies in competitive industries like insurance, law, online coupon shopping and other industries where the SEO competition is fierce all use **landing pages** to help get to the top of Google!

Landing pages, however, are not simply about "page tags." Rather, they are always "one click" from the home page, thereby leveraging the home page's SEO power to focus Google's attention on these highly valuable keywords. Behind the scenes, there are also link-building efforts for most successful landing pages.

Progressive Insurance

As an example, let's take a look at https://www.progressive.com/. Notice how the major product offerings are "one click" from the home page, and how the link structure reflects the target keywords. Of special import, scroll to the bottom of the page under "Insurance Offerings" and notice the links around target keyword phrases:

Car Insurance > links to /auto

Motorcycle Insurance > links to /motorcycle

Boat Insurance > links to /boat

Notice how each landing page mirrors a logical keyword phrase (not just "auto" but "auto insurance," not just "homeowners" but "homeowners insurance"), and is "one click" down from the home page. By "one click," we mean just that: go to the home page, and simply click once on these links: you then land on the defined landing page. Google, in turn, interprets these "one click" links as a major signal of a keyword's importance.

Also notice how Progressive has chosen five, *and only five*, of its most important product lines to feature via keyword-heavy links: *auto insurance, home insurance, motorcycle insurance, boat insurance*, and *commercial insurance*. Each is "one click" from the home page. This compares with other insurance lines (e.g., Segway Insurance, Golf Cart Insurance), which are "two clicks" from the home page via the "more choices" button.

Also notice if you View / Source to see the source code of Progressive.com's home page at https://www.progressive.com/, you'll see that the code for the landing page links is:

```
<div class="copy">

            <h3><a
href="https://www.progressive.com/motorcycle/">Motorcycle</
a></h3>

            <p>The #1 bike insurer, with rates as low
<span class="nowrap">as $75<sup>††</sup></span></p>

        </div>
```

Notice how this is an H3 (header) tag, that then goes to an A HREF (link) that is around the keyword *motorcycle*. So you have

Home Page > Link to the "motorcycle" landing page > around the keyword "motorcycle"

And, with just five major landing pages linked from the Home Page you have a very powerful signal as to what are the most important keyword phrases for the website: : *auto insurance, home insurance, motorcycle insurance, boat insurance,* and *commercial insurance.* And, scroll down to the footer, and notice how the footer also has links to these major landing pages.

Link Sculpting

This is called "link sculpting," and it is a very powerful way to "talk" to Google about your website's top priorities. Your **TODO**, therefore, is -

- **Link sculpt** "from" your Home Page "to" your landing pages around your target keywords.
- **Link sculpt** "from" your footer "to" your landing pages around your target keywords.

Structurally, therefore, here are your steps:

- **Identify** five or fewer major product lines that "match" your priority keyword phrases for SEO. These should be indicated on your **keyword worksheet** on the *landing page* tab.
- **Build** keyword-heavy, SEO-friendly **landing pages** for each product line.
- Make these "**one click**" from the home page via specific target keyword phrases as well as "**one click**" from a keyword-heavy footer on all pages.
- Relegate secondary product lines to a "**two click**" structure: home page > gateway page> other landing pages.

Check out Progressive's "gateway" page at http://jmlinks.com/5y. Other sites that use this structure are http://www.morenoranches.com, http://www.industrialfansdirect.com, and https://www.westpawdesign.com/. Notice how each has defined landing pages, and each has "one click" links from the home page to the defined landing pages.

Landing Page SEO

Each landing page should follow the principles of Page Tag SEO: weaving the target keywords strategically into the major tags, such as the TITLE tag, HEADER tags, IMG ALT tags, A HREF tag as well as having strong, well-written, keyword-dense content.

For example, click from the phrase links on the Progressive home page down to a landing page. I like to use the "motorcycle insurance" landing page as an example. So click from Progressive's home page to https://www.progressive.com/motorcycle/.

Notice how it is keenly SEO optimized for the target phrase "motorcycle insurance" plus helper words like "quote." You can see this clearly from its TITLE tag which is:

```
<title>Motorcycle Insurance: Motorcycle Insurance Quotes - Progressive</title>
```

If you "right click," and view the source in HTML, you'll notice the correct use of the META DESCRIPTION, HEADER tags, and A HREF cross-link around keyword phrases.

In addition, read the text out loud and you will notice heavy density for "motorcycle insurance" and related phrases. For a model SEO-friendly landing page, you can do no better!

My only critique would be that the page lacks an IMAGE with the IMG ALT reinforcing the keyword target.

For most websites, a good rule of thumb is to identify three to ten priority landing pages, which will each be laser focused on a single target keyword phrase and be "one click" from the home page and from the footer paragraph or navigation.

Localized Landing Pages

If your business has a local element, it is often useful to create localized landing pages for individual cities or towns that are "helper words" for your keywords. For example, Stamford Uniform and Linen (http://www.stamfordlinen.com/) wants to dominate Google not only for keyword phrases such as "Stamford Linen Service" (where the business is located) but for those in nearby towns, such as "Hartsdale Linen Service" or "Greenwich CT Linen Service." One method to accomplish this is **localized landing pages**.

Check out the company's home page, scroll to the bottom and notice the "one click" links to landing pages for target cities plus the keyword search "uniform rental service." For example, the Hartsdale page at http://www.stamfordlinen.com/Hartsdale/. Also notice how each landing page is unique, with content at the bottom of each city that is unique and different from the others in the set. Try some Google searches such as "Stamford Linen Service," "Hartsdale Linen Service," or "Greenwich CT Linen Service" to see how effective localized landing pages can be!

Another site that uses this effectively is Jonathan D. Sands. Check out his site map at http://jmlinks.com/13q. You'll see localized landing pages for cities such as Larchmont, Mamaroneck, and New Rochelle reflecting localized search patterns such as "Larchmont Personal Injury Lawyer" or "Mamaroneck Personal Injury Lawyer." Mr. Sands office is actually located in Mamaroneck, NY, but his SEO is trying to capture localized search patterns for nearby cities.

Doorway Pages and Localized Landing Pages

Caution: localized landing pages can be considered "doorway" pages by Google, especially post-Panda. You can read the official Google perspective on doorway pages at http://jmlinks.com/6a. The trick for localized landing pages is:

- **Be conservative**: create only a few landing pages for specific cities. Less is more.
- Make sure each has **unique** and valuable **content**.
- **Imagine you are a Googler** reading this page: does it seem to have a reason to exist, other than being optimized for SEO?

To see a company that has gone overboard on this tactic, visit http://www.certstaff.com. For example, go to http://jmlinks.com/6h and scroll to the bottom: you'll see page upon page of city-specific landing pages. This is a dangerous tactic, and sets that company up to be penalized, and completely removed from Google. Be careful! Less is more!

A good tactic is to give "driving directions" from various cities to your home office, therefore giving each city-specific page a reason to exist and making it read as useful for humans. At the same time, you can optimize it for SEO. Localized landing pages are close to violating Google's policy against doorway pages, so please create them at your own risk.

VIDEO. Watch a video tutorial on SEO landing pages at http://jmlinks.com/5z.

Moderation in All Things (Aristotle)

Here is one of the trade-offs of SEO: if you are too *aggressive*, you'll anger Google. But if you are too *passive*, you'll never get to the top. Remember: Google writes the rules to frighten people from doing anything (other than advertising on AdWords).

Speed a little, but don't be the fastest car on the Interstate.

So, don't overdo localized landing pages, and to every extent possible, make them unique, different, and useful to the human reader!

▶▶ DELIVERABLE: A LANDING PAGE LIST

Inventory your existing or to-be-created landing pages to reflect your major keyword patterns as described in your **keyword worksheet**. Using the "website structure worksheet" in combination with your **keyword worksheet**, create a list of your high priority landing pages. Each page will then be optimized via page tags and ultimately "one click" from the home page, using a keyword heavy syntax. I recommend a tab on your keyword worksheet that identifies no more than ten SEO-friendly landing pages for your website.

▶ WRITE A KEYWORD-HEAVY FOOTER

Another tactic I recommend is to write a **keyword-heavy footer**. Take a look at Progressive.com, scroll to the bottom, and check out their footer. Notice how the footer has direct links to major pages, all around the phrase "insurance" as in "motorcycle insurance." Or, take a look at my site https://www.jasonmcdonald.org/ or https://www.westpawdesign.com/. Again, scroll to the bottom and see that target SEO keywords have been embedded in the footer with direct links to landing pages.

Here's a screenshot of the West Paw Design footer, with arrows indicating the "one click" link to keyword-specific landing pages:

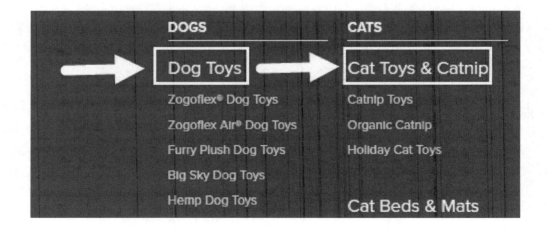

Your keyword footer should be short, well-written, and contain only your most important keywords. Link FROM the keyword footer TO your target landing pages. The footer increases the site-wide density of your website for your target keywords and allows for "link sculpting" – linking around strategic keywords to your key landing pages.

Using your Keyword Worksheet and the "landing pages" tab, make sure that as you create new pages for your website as well as blog pages that you link FROM these pages TO your landing pages around keyword-specific phrases. Again, do not overdo this. Just as a general rule, cross-link your pages to each other around important keyword phrases.

≫ CREATE A BLOG, AND START BLOGGING

Once you have your basic structure of Home Page > Landing Pages, and Footer > Landing Pages, it's time to create a blog. Blogs are critical for both SEO and for social media marketing, as a good keyword-heavy blog allows you to comment on keywords that matter to you and your customer. In terms of social media marketing, a blog gives you a place to put content that is of interest to your human readers and customers (See my *Social Media Marketing Workbook* on Amazon at http://jmlinks.com/smm for more on this topic).

In terms of SEO, a blog allows you to do the following:

1. A blog allows you to write short SEO-friendly posts on **long tail keywords**. Take a look at the West Paw Design blog at https://www.westpawdesign.com/scoop/. Notice how the company blogs on topics of interest to pet owners, and also optimizes its blog posts on keyword topics such as "Dog Friendly National Parks" (http://jmlinks.com/13r). Also notice how the blog links over to key landing pages, especially those that are product-oriented. Or, take a look at the Mentor Graphics blogs at https://www.mentor.com/blogs/ and notice how that hi-tech company uses its blogs to write engineering articles yet touch on keywords that matter to it such as "Sensor Modeling and Signal Conditioning Circuit Design" (esoteric keywords for a techie industry) (http://jmlinks.com/13s).

2. A blog gives "freshness" to your website, with Google rewarding sites that have frequent postings. Indeed, I recommend that you automate your home page so that it constantly rotates your three most recent blog posts onto the home page as at https://jm-seo.org/. Scroll down to "News and blogs" to see my most recent three blog posts.

3. A blog allows you to link "up" to your strategic landing pages, and pass "freshness" to those landing pages. Your landing pages will not change frequently, but by blogging on related topics you can communicate to Google that you are fresh and alive. For an example of this, read my blog post on "Hands on Marketing" at http://jmlinks.com/6g. In this way, your landing pages benefit

from "one click" links from the home page, from the keyword footer, and from rotating, fresh blog posts.

Blogs are covered in Chapter 4.1 on content, but in terms of website structure, realize that having a blog and posting SEO-friendly, keyword-heavy content to your blog on a regular basis is a "must" for success at search engine optimization. I recommend you commit to at least four blog posts per month on your keyword themes.

» USE KEYWORD HEAVY URLS OVER PARAMETER URLS

URLs or web addresses are what you see in the URL or address bar at the top of the browser. Google pays a lot of attention to URLs; URLs that contain target keywords clearly help pages climb to the top of Google. Here's a screenshot of the Progressive landing page URL for "Motorcycle Insurance":

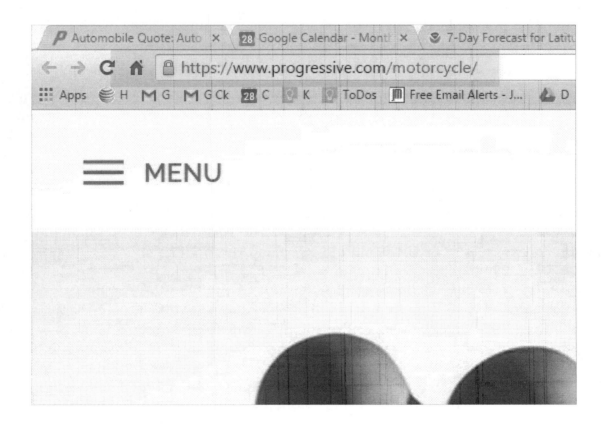

I have highlighted the URL in yellow.

Try a few competitive Google searches such as "Reverse Mortgage Calculator" (http://jmlinks.com/13t) and notice how the URLs that are on page one often contain the target keywords. Here's the #1 result for "Reverse Mortgage Calculator" at http://www.reversemortgage.org/About/Reverse-Mortgage-Calculator and here's the #3 result at http://reversemortgagealert.org/reverse-mortgage-calculator/.

What's the take-away? If possible, choose a **domain** that contains your target keywords. Beyond that, make sure that your URLs (**file names**) contain the target keywords.

Consider these two examples:

> **Example 1 / Geek File Name** - *http://www.yourcompany.com/files/ llk1/2/kyoklaol.html*. No "clues" to Google as to what is "contained" inside these directories and files.

> **Example 2 / English File Name** - *http://www.sf-attorney.com/medical-malpractice/obstetrics.html*. The domain, directories, and file names all indicate that this is a medical malpractice attorney, specializing in suing OB/GYN doctors.

By the way, what goes for URLs also goes for **images**: name your images after keywords just as you name your URLs after keywords. Rather than naming an image "image215.jpg" have your graphic designer name your images after your keywords such as "medical-malpractice.jpg."

Re-read the *Google SEO Starter Guide* (http://jmlinks.com/googleseo) and you'll notice that Google says, "Improve the structure of your URLS" (pg. 8) and "Optimize your use of images" (Pg. 18), so – again – just be crazy and do what Google is literally telling you to do: put keywords in your URLS and IMAGE file names / alt tags.

As part of the **DELIVERABLE** for Step #3, conduct an inventory of your website URLs and image file names (as well as ALT attributes). Are they keyword heavy? Do the visible keywords match the keyword themes from your keyword worksheet?

Parameter URLS

Just as important, **avoid parameter URLs**. Parameter URLs are URLs that contain numeric, crazy, geeky codes such as the question mark (?), percent sign (%), equals sign (=), or SessionIDs (often marked SESSID=), these indicate to Google that these are "temporary" pages not worth indexing. Static, keyword heavy URL's far outperform URLs that tell Google a website is database-driven via geeky parameter URLs.

PARAMETER URLs =
KISS OF (SEO) DEATH

As examples of sites that use parameter URLs, visit http://www.zilog.com or http://dl.acm.org. Both sites have URL's full of session IDs, question markets, etc. Refer back to the *Google SEO Starter Guide* (http://jmlinks.com/googleseo) and read the section on Parameter URLs. On page 8, Google says:

> URLs like (1) can be confusing and unfriendly. Users would have a hard time reciting the URL from memory or creating a link to it. Also, users may believe that a portion of the URL is unnecessary, especially if the URL shows many unrecognizable parameters. They might leave off a part, breaking the link. Some users might link to your page using the URL of that page as the anchor text. If your URL contains relevant words, this provides users and search engines with more information about the page than an ID or oddly named parameter would (2).

Here's an example URL on Zilog.com:

http://zilog.com/index.php?option=com_product&task=product&businessLine =1&id=77&parent_id=77&Itemid=57

To Google, that URL looks like a mess of information; therefore, this page is going to receive a negative ding in the search algorithm for its target keywords.

Avoid parameter URLs at all costs as Google severely deprecates them in its search results!

If you do have parameter based URLs, **insist** that your webmaster convert them to "pseudo static" URLs. You can Google "pseudo static" URLs for articles on this topic. If you are using WordPress make sure that the "permalink" setting has keyword-heavy URL's.

≫ LEVERAGE THE HOME PAGE FOR ONE CLICK LINKS

Google interprets your home page as the most powerful page on your website, and as we saw in the Page Tags chapter, you want to have lots of keyword-heavy text on the home page. In addition, you should embed our most important keywords into the home page TITLE tag. Beyond that, you should leverage your home page as a "one click" gateway to your landing pages. It's as if your HTML communicated this message to Google:

```
Home Page > One Click to Landing Pages = Hey Google! These
keywords are important to us!
```

Google also looks at the directory structure, namely the presence of keywords in URLs and how "far" those URLs are from the home page or "root" directory. So, in addition to naming your directories and files after your keyword families and high priority keywords, and placing "one click" links from your home page, create a directory structure that is "**shallow**" or "**flat**."

http://www.yourcompany.com/medical-malpractice/sue-doctors.html   (2nd level)

is seen by Google as "more important" than

http://www.yourcompany.com/1/files/new/medical-malpractice/sue-doctors.html (5th level)

Thirdly, your home page needs to communicate "freshness" to Google by having at least three *fresh* press releases and/or three new blog posts. Having new, fresh content that is "one click" from the home page signals to Google that your website is alive and updated (vs. a stagnant site that might be out of business), so it's a best practice to rotate press releases and/or blog posts through the home page as "one click" links.

> **VIDEO.** Watch a video tutorial on SEO-friendly home pages at http://jmlinks.com/18g.

▶ JOIN GOOGLE (AND BING) WEBMASTER TOOLS

Google rewards websites that make its job easier! Set up sitemaps for Google (and Bing), and participate in their official programs for Webmasters. Sign up for Google Webmaster Tools (now called the "Search Console") for your website (http://jmlinks.com/6c) as well as Bing Webmaster tools (http://jmlinks.com/6d). Then follow the steps below to alert Google to your Google-friendly files as follows.

First, create an **HTML site map** that makes it easy for a search engine spider to go from Page 1 to Page 2 to Page 3 of your website. If you use Javascript / CSS pull downs for navigation, your HTML site map is a critical alternative path for Google to index your website. Second, use the free tool at http://jmlinks.com/6e to create your XML site map. If you are using WordPress, look for a plugin that creates an HTML sitemap as well as an XML sitemap. Third, create a robots.txt file that points to your XML sitemap. (Note: if you are using WordPress, just search popular plugins for XML sitemaps and robots.txt functionality).

Fourth, after you have created these files, submit your **sitemap.xml** file via Webmaster tools. Pay attention as well to your "crawl errors" and "HTML suggestions." All things being equal, sites that participate in Webmaster tools will beat out sites that do not. Here's a screen shot of how to submit an XML sitemap via Google webmaster tools:

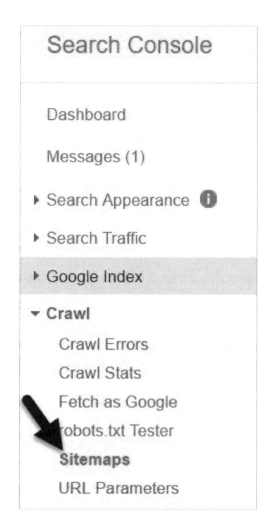

Login to your Search Console, then click on Crawl > Sitemaps. Next click on the red "Submit Sitemap" box on the far right to submit your XML sitemap.

Fetch as Google

Another feature available in the Google search console is "fetch as Google" located at Search Console > Crawl > Fetch as Google. What it does is alert Google to new or revised content on your website, thus increasing the speed at which your site gets indexed in Google and is available to rank high.

If you create a new page on your website, or edit an existing page, for example, you can login to the Google search console and "submit" your new URL to Google. In this way, you get into the Google index faster and can more quickly climb to the top of Google. Here's a screenshot:

This feature is also useful to get a new blog post indexed. First, write a new blog post. Second, log in to Google Search Console, and go to "Fetch as Google." Third, submit your URL to Google. This accelerates the indexing of a timely post to your blog.

To find out if content is indexed, use the *site:* command on Google. Enter a URL of your website after site: (no space) on Google. To see an example, go to http://jmlinks.com/13u which confirms that the blog post at https://www.jm-seo.org/2016/08/google-local-impness-description/ is "in" the Google index. If not, then I could use "fetch as Google" to alert Google to index / reindex it.

Set a Preferred Domain

You should also set a "preferred" domain (available under the gear icon, top right of the screen, under "site settings."). This is because you want to tell Google to use https://www.jm-seo.org/ not http://jm-seo.org. This prioritizes one format for SEO. Here's a screenshot:

Site Settings

Preferred domain
- ○ Don't set a preferred domain
- ○ Display URLs as **www.jm-seotips.org**
- ● Display URLs as **jm-seotips.org**

Crawl rate
- ● Let Google optimize for my site **(recommended)**
- ○ Limit Google's maximum crawl rate

Similarly, via your Web hosting company, make sure that the one you do NOT want redirects to the one you do want. For example, if you go to https://jm-seo.org/, it redirects you to https://www.jm-seo.org/. The magic word here is the "htaccess" file, which you can read about at http://jmlinks.com/6f. Generally, I'd ask your resident computer nerd or the tech support at your web hosting company to make sure one, and only one, format is in use.

Other Todos in Webmaster Tools

There are some other features of value in Webmaster tools. Scrolling down the left menu in Google Search Console, let me point out the following:

Messages. If you are penalized by Google (or Bing), you may see a warning message when you log in. Plus, you can be emailed alerts for web problems such as manual penalties or hacking.

Search Appearance. Drill down into some information about how Google sees your website structure, including so-called "microdata."

Search Traffic. Google will give you some data about which keywords you rrank for, as well as links to your site from other sites. In addition, it has a "mobile usability" check up feature to give suggestions as to how friendly your website is to mobile users.

Google Index. Here, you get information on how indexed your site is by Google, content keywords and other visibility into how Google perceives your website. Content keywords is a good checkup as you should see your top keywords on this list, high at the top.

Crawl. Google gives you information on how it is crawling your website, including errors as well as the important "fetch as Google" function described above.

Security Issues. If you've been hacked, Google will alert you and give you tips on how to recover.

Bing's Webmaster tools has similar features. In particular, Bing's information on inbound links to your site and keyword discovery tools are meritorious as is Bing's SEO Analyzer which gives feedback on how SEO-friendly a URL is.

VIDEO. Watch a video tutorial of how to use Google Webmaster Tools (Search Console) at http://jmlinks.com/17u.

▷▷ DELIVERABLE: A COMPLETED WEBSITE STRUCTURE WORKSHEET

At this point, you have the major components of the chapter **DELIVERABLE**: a **website audit** using the "website structure worksheet," namely:

1. **Your target landing pages**. These are your product or service pages that match common keywords searches your customers do on Google. Inventory the ones that you have as well as the ones that you need to create, and then outline the SEO-friendly content you will write (or rewrite) and weave into the correct tag structure.
2. **Your Blog.** You've set up a blog, and started to blog on your keywords.
3. **Your URL structure**. Avoid parameter (numeric, special character) based URLs in favor of keyword heavy URLs, and build a "shallow" website organization.
4. **Your Google-Friendly Files**. Make sure you've signed up for Google (and Bing) webmaster tools and Google Analytics.

5. **Participation in Google (and Bing) Webmaster Tools**. You should have registered for Webmaster Tools and crossed your t's and dotted your i's in terms of sitemaps (both XML and HTML) and preferred domain.

DELIVERABLE. Complete the "website structure worksheet." For the worksheet, go to https://www.jm-seo.org/workbooks (click on "SEO Fitness 2017," and enter the code '2017fitness' to register if you have not already done so), and click on the link to the "Website Structure Worksheet."

SURVEY OFFER

CLAIM YOUR $10 REBATE OR FREE BOOK! HERE'S HOW –

10. Visit http://jmlinks.com/survey.
11. Take a short, simple survey about the book.
12. Indicate whether you want a $10.00 rebate or a free copy of one of Jason's other books on SEO / Social Media Marketing / Job Search & Career-building.

WE WILL THEN –

- Rebate you the $10.00, or send you a free copy of one of the other books.

~ $10 REBATE OFFER ~

~ LIMITED TO ONE PER CUSTOMER ~

EXPIRES: 3/1/2017

SUBJECT TO CHANGE WITHOUT NOTICE

GOT QUESTIONS? CALL 800-298-4065

3.3

SEO Audit

SEO, like physical fitness, is all about results. It doesn't matter how much you *know* about physical fitness if you don't *do* anything about it! Similarly, in SEO, it doesn't matter how much you *know* about SEO if you don't *do* SEO! So before we turn to tactics such as content marketing and "off page" SEO, this chapter is a *review* and a **Todo**. It's a moment to stop, review what you've learned so far, and make sure you've completed the required worksheets. It's time to audit your website for On Page SEO best practices, and to start *doing* SEO.

Remember, to access the worksheets, go to https://www.jm-seo.org/workbooks (click on "SEO Fitness 2017," and enter the code '2017fitness' to register if you have not already done so), and click on each worksheet.

Let's get started!

Todo List:

- » Deliverable: A Keyword Audit

- » Deliverable: A Page Tag Audit

- » Deliverable: A Home Page Audit

- » Deliverable: A Website Structure Audit

» Deliverable: a Keyword Audit

SEO, as we have learned, begins with **keywords**. Verify that you know, in a very specific way, the following:

- **Keyword search patterns.** Different customers search in different ways, and keywords self-organize into logical keyword groups. Each keyword group has a core keyword (e.g., "motorcycle insurance") with helper keywords (e.g., "quote," "rate," "cheap") plus some close synonyms (e.g., "motorbike," "moped," "Harley Davidson"). Do you know your **keyword patterns**? Are they written down in specific terms on your **keyword worksheet**?

- **Keyword Volume.** Smart SEO experts *fish where the fish are*: they target keywords that have the highest search **volumes**. Using the Google AdWords Keyword Planner, have you researched which keywords have the highest volumes in your industry?

- **Keyword Value.** It's not just about *volume*; it's also about *value*, especially *value to you* and your business. The Keyword Planner gives you useful data on the CPC (cost-per-click) bid in AdWords, but it's up to you to identify "riches in the niches," the very specific searches that are of high **value** to your sales funnel. Which keywords are most likely to be a customer ready to buy, or at least ready to fill out a feedback or inquiry form?

Your **keyword audit DELIVERABLE** consists of sitting down with your management or marketing / sales team members and filling out a detailed, and organized **keyword worksheet**. As part of this process, measure your rank on Google to set a **baseline** of where your company stands in terms of target Google search queries using SEO Book's RankChecker for Firefox or a paid rank-checking tool such as Moz.com or Ahrefs.com.

> **VIDEO.** Watch a quick video tutorial on how to build out your keyword worksheet at http://jmlinks.com/17m.

≫ DELIVERABLE: A PAGE TAG AUDIT

Now that you know your keywords, where do you put them? **Page Tags**, of course. Here are the elements of a Page Tag Audit, proceeding page by page:

- **What is the logical keyword focus of each page, especially your landing pages?** Leaving aside the very special home page, each page on your website should have a tight, logical keyword focus. Conduct an inventory of all pages on your site, and cross-match each page to a logical, tight keyword query on Google that it can successfully target. Next, audit whether the current tags of that page contain the target keyword. Remember, the best SEO page tag structure is:

- o **Home Page:** embed your most important keyword phrases in the TITLE tag, a strong Meta Description tag, visible content that contains your keywords, and "one click" links down to specific landing pages. (*See below for specific instructions for the home page*).
- o **Landing Pages:** a strong website should have between five and ten landing pages, reflecting the "core keywords" on your keyword worksheet. These generally reflect your company's primary keyword patterns.
- o **Keyword Footer:** write a keyword-heavy footer, and include "one click" links from keywords in your footer to your target landing pages.
- o **A Blog:** use your blog for long-tail keywords and/or micro keywords, and click "up" to your target landing pages.
- **Meta Tag Audit.** The two meta tags that really matter, of course, are the TITLE and META DESCRIPTION tag. Inventory the existing tags vs. suggested improvements to the TITLE and META DESCRIPTION tags on *all pages* (include blog posts and product pages), not just your home page and landing pages.
- **Tag Audit.** Besides the META TAGS, the A HREF, HEADER, and IMG ALT tags are important. Inventory your existing tags vs. the suggested tag improvements across all pages. Pay special attention to the A HREF tag and how links are "sculpted" between pages around your target keywords.

Having looked at tag structure, turn next to the **content** on each page of your website. As we have learned, Google likes keyword-heavy content that is nonetheless written in high quality, natural syntax English. Inventory each page to verify that it has SEO-friendly content that matches the keyword target. Be sure to include related and adjacent search terms to avoid a "Panda penalty" for low quality content. Write using complete sentences, good grammar, and related terms for your target keywords.

The purpose of the **Page Tag audit** is to compare / contrast your pages with SEO best practices to verify that your website as a whole communicates your keyword themes to Google (and Bing, too). Don't forget to audit both *existing* pages and pages that are *TBD* ("to be done") as identified in your keyword research. Begin to make a plan to write and deploy new landing pages that you may have identified as missing in your website architecture.

VIDEO. Watch a quick video tutorial on how to conduct a Page Tag audit at http://jmlinks.com/6j.

▶ DELIVERABLE: A HOME PAGE AUDIT

Your **home page** is the most important page of your website for SEO performance, so spend a lot of time working on its content, images, and links. It's worth special attention. A good home page audit works as follows:

Target Keywords. Reviewing your keyword worksheet, what are your most *important*, most *competitive* keywords? Use your powerful home page TITLE tag to convey to Google your website's primary keyword theme, and remember it must be less than eighty characters, with only about 59 visible on Google.

Meta Tags. Review and revise not only your TITLE tag but also your META DESCRIPTION tag, including high priority keywords and making sure that you respect the META DESCRIPTION character limit of 155 characters.

Home Page Content. Google pays a lot of attention to the text on your home page, so verify that the keywords on your keyword worksheet actually appear at least once on your home page. At the same time, do not clutter your home page so much that it doesn't look good "for humans." *The art of SEO is to combine the keyword heavy text that Google likes, with the pretty visuals that humans like.* This is especially true for the home page, so put pictures, graphics, and actions at the top of the page, and keyword heavy text for Google at the bottom.

One Click to Landing Pages. Make sure to have "one click" links down from your home page to your priority landing pages, so inventory whether a) your landing pages exist (if not create them), and b) whether they are "one click" from the home page.

VIDEO. Watch a quick video tutorial on how to conduct a Home Page audit at http://jmlinks.com/18g.

▶ DELIVERABLE: A WEBSITE STRUCTURE AUDIT

As we learned in Chapter 3.2 on **Website Structure**, there are do's and don'ts for structural SEO:

Do include keywords in your URLs. Are your existing URL's keyword heavy? Do your domains, directories, file names and even graphic names contain keywords?

Don't use parameter URLs. Inventory your existing URLs and look for question marks (?), percentage signs (%), and session IDs. All are very negative for SEO, and if they exist, have your webmaster or programmer transition to static or *pseudostatic* URLs as soon as possible.

Do sculpt your links. A strong SEO website uses internal link syntax to talk to Google. Your home page should have keyword heavy "one click" links down from the home page to your landing pages. Similarly, your site navigation should be keyword heavy and "sculpt" your links around keyword phrases, and your blog should have "one click" links up to your major landing pages around the target keyword phrases.

Finally, make sure that your website contains your **Google friendly files**, especially a robots.txt file, an XML sitemap, and an HTML sitemap. Every page should link to the HTML sitemap, and the HTML sitemap in turn should have keyword-heavy links to all derivative pages. This important file makes it easy for the Googlebot to crawl your website.

Join **Google Search Console (Webmaster Tools)** to be part of the Google "Mickey Mouse Club" and get insider information on how Google perceives your website! For extra credit, join *Bing Webmaster Tools*, as well.

Now that you've completed these **DELIVERABLES**, it's time to move to our next step, **Step #4: Create Content**.

4.1

CONTENT SEO

In **Step #1**, you defined your goals; in **Step #2**, you identified your keywords; and in **Step #3**, you structured your pages and website to talk to Google about your target keywords. In **Step #4**, you begin to populate your SEO-friendly website with keyword heavy content.

Content, after all, is king.

But let's be clear. Just throwing content up on your website willy-nilly won't help your SEO! Why? Well, for one, we've already learned that *well structured content* (SEO-friendly page tags, SEO-friendly website structure) is critical for success at SEO. For two, that content needs to be well-written and include your keywords in sufficient density. And, for three, Google increasingly looks at not only grammar and related words but whether the human user actually finds it interesting, so you need to write content that's good for Google AND good for humans.

In **Step #4**, we will expand on this by creating an **SEO Content Marketing Strategy** ("Content SEO" for short) built upon your keyword targets.

Content SEO is all about creating web pages that *match* Google search *queries* with compelling, relevant *content,* be that on a specific web page, a press release, or a blog post. **Content SEO** is all about creating an on-going "content marketing machine" (*daily, weekly, monthly content*) that produces compelling SEO-friendly content for your website. And, in the new synergy between SEO and *social media marketing*, **Content SEO** is also about creating content that real people want to read, and want to share on Twitter, LinkedIn, Facebook, Google+ and other social networks.

Let's get started!

TODO LIST:

>> Identify Keyword Themes

» Create a Content Map

» Set up a Blog

» Create a Content Marketing Plan

»» Deliverable: A Content Marketing Plan

» IDENTIFY KEYWORD THEMES

Every successful website has keyword **themes** just as every successful company or organization has a **focus**. You don't produce *everything*, nor do your target searchers search Google for *everything*. You **focus**, and they **focus**. If you are Safe Harbor CPAs (http://www.safeharborcpa.com/), a CPA firm in San Francisco, for example, your target customers search Google for things like "San Francisco CPA Firms," "Business CPAs in San Francisco, CA," or keyword specific searches such as "CPA Firm for IRS Audit Defense in SF," or "FBAR Tax Issues." Guess what? Safe Harbor CPAs has matching content on its website for each of those queries, including an active blog, and that's no accident!

If you are a Houston probate attorney, you'll need lots of content about "Houston" and about "probate" plus related terms like estate planning, guardianships, and wills. Take a look at http://www.fordbergner.com/ and – guess what – that site has well-optimized content, including an up-to-date blog, on exactly those keyword themes.

If **keyword discovery** is about organizing your SEO strategy around keyword themes, then **Content SEO**, in turn, is about creating a strategy to produce the type of content that "matches" your keyword themes on an on-going basis.

MATCH CONTENT

TO SEARCH QUERIES

The first step is to match your keyword themes as identified on your keyword worksheet with content that needs to be produced. Among the most common themes are:

Branded or Navigational Searches. Searches in which customers already know your company, and simply use Google to find you quickly. In the example of Safe Harbor CPAs, a branded Google search is literally "Safe Harbor CPAs," while for Ford Bergner Law Firm it is "Ford Bergner." **Matching content**: your "about you" page on the website.

Reputational Searches. Customers often research reviews about a company, product, or service online before making that final decision to make a purchase. Google your company name plus "reviews" and make sure that what they see about your company is positive; you'll be creating and encouraging content to proliferate positive content about your company's reputation. **Matching content**: people don't search for *testimonials* about a business; they search for *reviews*. So rename your *testimonials* page on your website to *reviews* for better SEO.

Anchor Searches. These are searches in which a core customer *need* matches a core *product or service*. In the example of Safe Harbor CPAs, an anchor search would be "San Francisco CPA Firms," or "Tax Preparation San Francisco." For a large company like Progressive Insurance, the anchor searches are "Auto Insurance" or "Motorcycle Insurance." **Matching content**: your landing pages.

> **Educational Anchor Pages**. Besides transactional keyword searches, there are often common and repeated "educational searches" for which people want long form content. An example would be an explanation of the difference between *follicular unit extraction* and *follicular unit transplantation* as techniques for hair transplants. Or, another example would be an explanation of *how to contest a will under Oklahoma law*. **Matching content**: FAQ (Frequently Asked Questions) documents, eBooks, and long-form blog posts.

Keyword Specific Searches / Long Tail. Searches that are usually (but not always) long tail searches (multiple search keywords), and reflect a very focused customer need. For example, "IRS Audit Defense CPA in San Francisco" or "motorcycle insurance quotes online" vs. just "CPA Firm." **Matching content**: blog posts.

Keyword Specific Searches / Micro Searches. Short but micro-focused search queries such as "Tag Heuer Repair," or "Breitling Repair," or "AdWords Coupons." These are short but very specific search queries. **Matching content**: blog posts.

News and Trending Searches. These are searches reflecting industry news, trends, and buzz. For example, with recent IRS initiatives to crack down on overseas assets, a search such as "FBAR" reflects an awareness of foreign asset disclosure requirements. Similarly, if you were a networking company, growing awareness of computer security would make blog posts on "cybersecurity" a good bet to attract interested customers. **Matching content**: blog posts, press releases, and video summaries (with matching YouTube videos)

These are not the only types of keyword queries and matching content that might exist; just the most common. Your **TODO** here is to track trending topics, and blog on them quickly to "get ahead" of the news cycle. Use tools like Google Alerts (https://www.google.com/alerts) and Buzzsumo (http://www.buzzsumo.com) to monitor trending topics in your industry.

Evergreen Content and Link-bait Content

Many SEO content experts also distinguish between *evergreen* keywords (keywords that are always valuable such as "CPA San Francisco") vs. *time-sensitive* content (such as "2015 Tax Changes). And don't forget the difference between *educational* search queries and *transactional* search queries ("knee pain" vs. "best knee surgeon in San Francisco"). Finally, there is *link bait* content (such as infographics, or tutorial posts), designed to attract links, and of course *social media content*, especially content that is designed to be highly shareable on networks like Facebook or Twitter. Brainstorm content that has a long shelf-life, and that will attract user interest and inbound links.

Here's a screenshot from Backlinko (http://jmlinks.com/18v) showing an "Evergreen" FAQ on how to build links for SEO:

Link Building: The Definitive Guide

Link building is the most important (and challenging) SEO skill. Actually, it's a culmination of several different skills: you need to master content creation, sales, programming, psychology, and good old-fashioned marketing if you want other people to consistently link to your site.

IF YOU'RE LOOKING FOR MORE SEARCH ENGINE TRAFFIC (AND WHO ISN'T?) THEN LINK BUILDING IS A MUST.

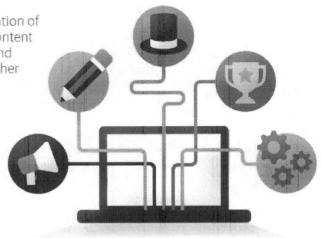

Regardless of the target keywords, the basic goal is to map out the types of content that are most relevant to you and your customers, and to start a content marketing process that generates highly relevant content on a regular basis. So your process is:

1. **Identify** a target keyword phrase, and match it to branded, educational, evergreen, anchor content, etc.
2. **Brainstorm** the type of content you need to produce that best matches the keyword query such as a long-form blog post, an FAQ document, or a short and quick blog about a trending topic.
3. **Produce** the content on a regular and systematic basis.
4. **Promote** the content, often by syndicating it as a Press Release, sharing it on social media, or even advertising it on Google, Facebook, or Twitter.

For your first **ToDo**, review your **keyword worksheet**, brainstorm your keyword patterns, and group your keyword families into patterns that reflect **branded search**,

reputational search, **anchor search**, **esoteric search**, and **news search** and other patterns.

» CREATE A CONTENT MAP

Now that you have your keyword themes, it's time to brainstorm the types of content you are going to create that will match the relevant keyword theme. Your second **TODO** is to create a **content map**. In a sense, you are "reverse engineering" the process of Google search: taking what people search on Google as your **end point**, and creating the type of content that has a good chance of appearing in Google search results as your **starting point**. Your **content map** will map your keyword themes to the relevant locations on your website.

Here's a table mapping out how keyword themes are generally reflected on website locations:

KEYWORD THEME	WEBSITE LOCATION	COMMENTS ON CONTENT SEO
Branded Searches	Home Page, About You, Testimonial Pages	Branded search is all about making sure you show up for your own name as well as commonly appended helper words like "reviews." Make sure that at least some TITLE tags communicate your name, and your "about" page is focused on branded search. Don't forget branded search for key company employees (JM Internet Group vs. Jason McDonald, for example).
Anchor Searches / Transactional Searches	Home Page, Landing Pages, Product Pages (High Level), FAQ documents, eBooks	Anchor or transactional search terms generally reflect your product categories in the format that customers search. Revisit *progressive.com*, for example, and you'll see how each anchor search query is reflected in a focused **landing page**. In addition, the site navigation and links are "sculpted" around keywords to pull Google up to the target landing pages. Besides landing pages, FAQ documents, Q&A documents, or infographics can match these anchor keywords.
Very Specific Searches	Product sub pages, blog posts.	Your esoteric searches are generally long tail searches, and/or searches for very niche, focused products or services ("micro" searches). These are less competitive than anchor searches and are well served by content on product sub pages as well as blog posts.
News Searches	Press releases, blog posts	Every industry has news, buzz, and timely topics! The place to put this content is

		generally either in a press release on your website, and/or a blog post.
Educational Searches	Blog posts, FAQ document, possible eBooks	These are when the potential customer is in "learn mode" as in the "causes of hair loss" rather than "Best Hair Transplant Surgeon in Miami."

For your second **TODO**, take your keyword themes and map out where they should be reflected on your website into your **content map**. I recommend doing this in Excel. Check your rank on Google searches vs. relevant search queries for each type – if you are not on page one, or not in the top three positions for a query... you have work to do! If possible, create a content or editorial calendar and divvy up who in your company will be responsible for writing which content. The goal is to make a "content marketing machine" so that you are constantly feeding fresh content to your website and to your social media. Think *factory production*, not *William Shakespeare*!

In some cases, you may have *missing* elements (for example, you don't have blog or don't produce press releases); in others you may have the elements there *already* (product specific pages, for example) but their content is not SEO-friendly (has poorly defined TITLE tags, content does not reflect logical keyword target, etc.). Regardless, you are mapping your keyword themes to the logical locations on your website with the goal of getting into a rhythm or content creation process of creating SEO-friendly content on a regular basis.

As you brainstorm content, keep an eye on social media. What types of content interests your customers? What types of content are they likely to share? Use a tool like Buzzsumo (http://www.buzzsumo.com/), input your keywords, and identify the most shared content on Facebook, Twitter, LinkedIn, etc. This tells you what type of content is popular, and therefore you can produce that content yourself.

Here's a screenshot from Buzzsumo showing the most shared article on "hair transplant" for the past year:

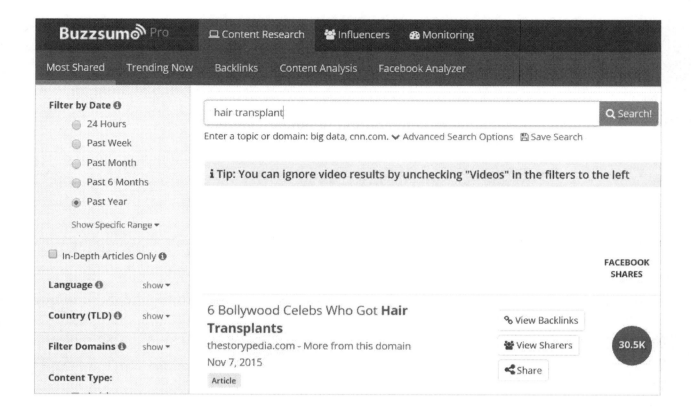

≫ SET UP A BLOG

To succeed at SEO, you must have a blog! Blogs are great for social media marketing, and for SEO, your blog helps in these important ways:

- **Micro-specific Content**. Whereas your major landing pages must reflect "anchor" searches, your blog can have a nearly infinite number of pages tied together by keyword themes. Your blog gives you the easy ability to create a lot of content and match that content on the many small, fragmented and long-tail searches that make up today's search behavior. Often you might not win on the "major" searches but you can make up for this by winning on the "micro" searches, many of which will be low volume but high value. (In addition, your blog gives you content to share on social media).

- **Freshness**. Google rewards sites that have new, fresh content. Having a blog gives you an easy way to churn out fresh content and send a freshness signal to Google: we're alive, we're alive, we're alive... I recommend at least four blog posts per month for this reason, and rotating three blog posts on your home page as I do on https://jm-seo.org/.

- **Website Size**. Size matters (at least to Google)! (*Didn't see that joke coming, did you?*). Given the choice between *pizza restaurant* No. 1 with 10 web pages, and *pizza restaurant* No. 2 with 1000 pages, Google will prefer the larger website: *it must be more important because it has more content*. A blog allows you to expand the size your web content.

As for blogging platforms, the best, by far, is **WordPress**. If you do not already have a blog, touch base with your Web developer and insist that he or she set up a blog for you. Major providers such as GoDaddy have easy-to-use, out-of-the-box WordPress packages. As you blog on WordPress, be sure to "tag" each blog post with keyword themes that reflect your keyword targets (as identified on your keyword worksheet).

Take a look at our blog at http://jmlinks.com/15k for examples of best blogging practices for SEO, including tagging blog posts based on keyword themes. Here's a screenshot of our WordPress "tag cloud," located at the far left of every page on our blog:

```
TAGS
AdWords AdWords Books Arizona
Austin Book Reviews Books Business California
Content Marketing Directory Display
Network Free Tools Google Google Algorithm
Google Analytics Google Local Houston
Keyword Planner Keywords Local SEO
Los Angeles Marketing Metrics Mobile-friendly
Mobile SEO New York New York City
Photography Remarketing Retargeting San Francisco
SEO SEO Books SEO Tips SEO Training
Small Business Social Media Social
Media Marketing Texas Top
Tens Tucson Twitter Marketing Viral
Marketing WordPress SEO Yelp
```

Notice how our WordPress tags reflect our target keywords such as AdWords, SEO, and Social Media Marketing as indicated with a bigger font, meaning more blog content. To learn more about WordPress tags, please visit http://jmlinks.com/6n.

Blog Hosting

Note that it is better to host your blog on your own site (http://www.company.com/blog) than on another site (http://company.wordpress.com/). However, the "Perfect is the enemy of the Good" (Voltaire), so if you can't host on your own domain, host on another platform. For a quick blogging platform, I prefer Blogger (http://www.blogger.com) to WordPress.com (http://www.wordpress.com), as the former is very SEO-friendly while the latter (ironically) is not, and has many obnoxious lock-ins to prevent you from porting your blog to your own site at a later time. (Note: just to confuse you, *Wordpress.org* is the site for the free software (good), whereas *WordPress.com* is a revenue-generating site (bad)).

VIDEO. Watch a quick video tutorial on SEO-friendly blogging at http://jmlinks.com/17t vs. how to blog for social media marketing purposes at http://jmlinks.com/16p.

In a nutshell, a blog post that is *meant for SEO* is meant to be "searched for" and to assist you in propelling your website to the top of a relevant search query on Google; a blog post that is *meant for social media marketing,* in contrast, is aimed at being "shared" by real humans on sites like Facebook or Twitter. Both are important and valuable reasons why everyone needs a blog!

»» DELIVERABLE: A CONTENT MARKETING PLAN

Now that you have a **content map** of your website vs. your keyword themes on your **keyword worksheet**, you are ready to produce your **DELIVERABLE**: a **content marketing plan**. Your content marketing plan will consist of these basic phases.

Phase 1: Quick Fix. Based on your keyword worksheet including the content map, conduct an inventory of existing pages. Adjust their TITLE tags, META DESCRIPTION tags, and content to bring that content into alignment with your logical Google searches. I usually also write a "keyword paragraph" and place on all website pages to increase keyword density and allow for link sculpting. Don't forget to optimize the content of that all-important home page!

Phase 2: Content Inventory. Are you missing anything? Often times, there will be a very important keyword pattern that has no corresponding landing page, for example. Or your site will not have a blog, or you will have never set up a press release system. Inventory what you are missing and start to prioritize what needs to be done to get that content on your website. Commonly needed elements are:

- **Blog**. I recommend at least four blog posts per month; these can be on easy, man-on-the-street type themes but you really need to commit to at least four, and make sure that they are relevant vis-a-vis your keyword themes.
- **Press Releases**. As discussed in Chapter 4.2, I recommend at least two per month and (if possible), using the CISION / PRWEB system (http://www.prweb.com/) to syndicate them (cost is approximately $350 / month).
- **Landing Pages**. Make sure that each major search has a corresponding landing page. In addition to your transactional landing pages, make sure that you brainstorm educational searches and create long form content such as FAQ (Frequently Asked Questions) documents. These are great "link bait," i.e. ways to attract inbound links to your website.
- **Anchor Content**. Consider writing the "ultimate" guide to major topics in your industry, provocative "hot button" issues, and other timely topics. This type of content is great to a) attract links, and b) to acquire customer email addresses and contact information. Most companies need to commit to one, and only one, type of anchor content.

Phase 3: Content Creation Process. Once you have done the Quick Fix to the website and created any missing landing pages, set up a blog, and/or set up a press releases system, you need to create a content creation schedule and process. This is an assessment of who will do what, when, where, and how to create the type of on-going content that Google and Web searchers will find attractive.

WORKSHEETS. For your **DELIVERABLE**, fill out the "content marketing worksheet," specifically each phase. For the worksheet, go to https://www.jm-seo.org/workbooks (click on "SEO Fitness 2017," and enter the code '2017fitness' to register if you have not already done so), and click on the link to the "content marketing worksheet."

4.2

PRESS RELEASES

After you've created your landing pages, anchor or evergreen content, and begun to blog (See Chapter 4.3), it's time to shift gears towards *Off Page* SEO. Remember *Off Page* SEO is about freshness, links, and social mentions. (Review Chapter 1.3 on Off Page SEO for more information on *Off Page* SEO, or jump ahead to Chapter 5.1). Blogging gets you freshness, press releases get you freshness and links, and then we'll turn to link-building and social mentions in their own right in Chapters 5.1 and 5.2.

So, we'll begin with Press Releases. Formal **press releases** should be a major part of your **SEO Content** strategy. Why? Because Google rewards sites that have fresh content, and press releases get you easy inbound links.

Here are the reasons. First, websites that have new, fresh content (for example, a press release or blog post put up in the last week) are clearly more "alive" than websites that never get updated. We live in a fast-paced world, and users want the *latest* iPhone software, the *latest* news about Donald Trump, and the *latest* nutritional supplement. Google wants to give users the latest and greatest on any topic as well. Second, fresh content signals to Google that your website and business are still alive vs. the many "walking dead" websites that reflect businesses dead or dying in this age of recession. And third, press releases have a unique SEO advantage: **syndication**. Free and paid syndication services like PRLog.org or PRWeb.com connect with blogs, portals, other websites and even Twitter feeds to push your press releases across the Web, creating inbound buzz and backlinks which Google interprets as signs of community authority. Press release SEO, in short, gives a three-for-one benefit!

Let's get started!

TODO LIST:

>> What is a Press Release?

>> Make a Press Release Calendar

>> Upload Your SEO-Friendly Press Releases

>> Leverage Free Press Release Syndication Services

>> >> Deliverables: Press Release Worksheet

>> WHAT IS A PRESS RELEASE?

Have you ever heard the quip about the weather, that everyone talks about it, but no one does anything about it? Or, if you don't like the news, go out and make some of your own? Well, there's some truth in these adages: you need to toot your own (marketing) horn to be successful, and press releases allow this in spades.

But what is a press release, and how does it differ from a blog post? Think of a blog post (which we'll cover in more detail in the next Chapter) as a much shorter, more informal, off-the-cuff type of content vs. a more formal press release in which your company FORMALLY ANNOUNCES something NEW AND EXCITING. A common example would be when you launch a new product. If you're the Ford Motor Company, for instance, and you're announcing the new and improved 2018 Mustang, then it's time for a press release, usually written in the format of:

> *Detroit, Michigan* – *December 1, 2017. The Ford Motor Company, the leading producer of American-made sports vehicles, is proud to announce their new 2018 Mustang. With a venerable history as an American "muscle" car, the new 2018 Mustang will also be eco-friendly with its hybrid engine.*

> etc. etc.

> Basically Ford has some NEWS and it's ANNOUNCING that news to the world via press release.

You can browse sample press releases at http://jmlinks.com/13x and http://jmlinks.com/13y. Focus on those in your industry, and notice how company after company is "tooting its own horn" by announcing "news."

>> MAKE A PRESS RELEASE CALENDAR

What can make a good press release? **Almost anything.** Keep your keyword worksheet in mind and look for press release opportunities around your company, products, or services that match up with your SEO keyword targets. I recommend you create a **press release calendar** of opportunities.

Tip. Many people are too "shy" acting as if they and their company don't have any "legitimate" news. Don't be shy! If you don't toot your own horn, no one will toot it for you. And remember that for SEO purposes, we're really aiming our promotion at Google, so if "real people" read our press releases, that's great, but our real objective is to use press releases to influence Google to rank our website higher. If they influence Google, we're happy!

For your first **TODO**, open up a Word document, title it "Press Release Calendar," and write down a list of possible press release topics and dates of the release. For example:

SAMPLE PRESS RELEASE TOPIC:	WHEN TO RELEASE:
New product or service	Every time you have a new product or service, generate a press release.
Annual Trade Show	Generate a press release before the annual trade show, as well as after announcing your participation to celebrate your success.
Personnel Changes	Generate a press release for every major corporate hire.
New website content	Generate a press release after any major blog post, list of "top seven resources," infographic, etc., and even when you update a landing page or anchor content.
Partnership Announcements	Generate a press release after any cooperative partnership with a company or supplier.
Industry Awards or Milestones	Any time you win an industry award or cross a milestone (such as the 1000th follower on Twitter), it's time for a press release!

Your **press release calendar** will help keep you focused, and tie your press release opportunities to your keyword worksheet. The goal is to avoid writer's block and get into a rhythm of at least two press releases per month, minimum. Have a company meeting and divvy up the responsibilities by assigning writing a press release to different people in the company for different events, or for different months. Make your SEO a "team sport," rather than attempting to do it all yourself.

Steps to Writing an SEO-friendly Press Release

Once you have an idea in hand, here are the steps to create a press release:

1. Identify the **press release idea**. Realize that a press release can be not only a new product or a new technology but something as simple as your participation in a trade show, an event that you may be having, a new hire, new inventory, or even your commentary on an industry trend. **Literally, anything new can become a press release!**

2. Connect the press release idea to a **target keyword** from your keyword worksheet. The point of generating press releases, after all, is to improve keyword performance.

3. Create a **press release** using your SEO page template and follow "**SEO best practices**" for on page SEO (see below). Be sure to include your keywords in the Headline / Title, and in the actual content of the release itself.

4. **Upload** the press release to your website, be sure that your website has a press release section with each press release on an independent URL, and include a "one click" link from the home page to the press release.

5. Leverage free and/or paid **syndication services** such as PRLog.org and PRWeb.com to proliferate mentions of your press releases around the Internet.

►► UPLOAD YOUR SEO-FRIENDLY PRESS RELEASES

Double-check your press release to make sure that it follows "on page" SEO best practices. Here's your checklist:

ITEM	SEO PAGE TAG STRUCTURE
Pithy, exciting headline	<TITLE> tag
First paragraph with "main idea"	<META DESCRIPTION> tag and first paragraph. Include a link to your website in the first paragraph usually around a keyword phrase.

Target URL	A target URL on your website, to which you want to attract Google. Embed this in the first paragraph, and have it as a "naked" URL (http://) format in the third paragraph.
Several paragraphs describing your news and an image.	Write keyword heavy copy and include at least one image with ALT attribute.
Contact information for more info.	Embedded URL early in the press release, set up in http:// format plus contact information at the end of the release

In other words, follow your HTML page tag template to optimize your press release in terms of its on-page SEO. Be sure to embed your target keywords in your <TITLE> tag, and use best SEO practices like the H1 family, <B>, <STRONG>, ALT attributes, for images etc. Write **keyword-heavy** text for the press release body! Make sure that it has a snappy <TITLE> and a snappy META DESCRIPTION / first paragraph so that people will be interested in "reading more."

At the website structure level, your best practice is to have a directory called "news" as in *http://www.yourcompany.com/news/* and to host each press release in HTML linked to from a primary news gateway page. I also recommend that you run at least three press releases on your home page, with "one click" links down to each new press release. All of this freshens your website and pulls Google into your new content.

VIDEO. Watch a quick video tutorial on how to write an SEO-friendly press release at http://jmlinks.com/18f.

Good examples of press releases can be found http://jmlinks.com/13z and http://jmlinks.com/14a. Duct Tape Marketing has a nifty tool to help you write a press release at http://jmlinks.com/14b. Here's as screenshot:

Press Releases After the Penguin Update

Before the Penguin update to Google, you could use Press Releases to "optimize" your inbound links. For example, you'd create a bunch of press releases all linking back to your site around the phrase "industrial fans" or "motorcycle insurance." This manipulation did not make Google happy, so the search giant pressured the major services to add the NOFOLLOW tag to their releases, which nullified much of this benefit, as part of Google's so-called Penguin algorithm update.

Thus, for a short while, press releases had little impact on SEO. However, there is always another turn of the screw. Now, despite the fact that press release URL's remain "nofollow" in most circumstances, Google does tend to reward sites that issue them. (Trust me: I know this based on client experiments; the reason probably being that in many industries, Google has so few links to choose from among competing sites that the sheer quantity of press release links can be sufficient to help a site get to the top).

In addition, if you use ONLY the *http://* format for your clickable links, there are still a small percentage of sites that retain the DOFOLLOW link structure. So be sure to include links FROM the press release BACK to your site in the format of http://www.company.com. The reality is that Google is often forced to choose not between two GREAT sites to rank for a search query but between two just OK sites: if yours is the site with a few inbound links via Press Releases, including *nofollow* links, you can often win.

> *The perfect is the enemy of the good (Voltaire).*
>
> *You don't have to run faster than the bear, just faster than your buddy (Unknown).*
>
> *Google might publicly say one thing, but the reality might be something altogether different and this includes the value of nofollow links.*

To see examples of Press Releases issued by the JM Internet Group with examples of proper link formatting, visit http://jmlinks.com/6q.

>> LEVERAGE FREE PRESS RELEASE SYNDICATION SERVICES

Once you've created your press release and uploaded it to your own website, you are ready to leverage press release syndication services. The best **free** service is PRLog.org (http://www.prlog.org/) and the best **paid** service is PRWeb.com (http://www.prweb.com/), owned by Cision. You can learn more about the available packages from Cision at http://jmlinks.com/6s.

If you have budget, I highly recommend setting up a paid Cision account. With a yearly package, the cost per release is about $175. The paid service gets you many times the benefit of the free services like PRLog.org.

After you've set up your account on one of these services, open your press release in one browser window. In another window, log into the press release syndication service and begin the process of submitting a release. Copy and paste the following from your press release into the syndication service -

Headline. Make sure it includes your target keywords!

Quick Summary. Write a pithy, exciting one-to-two sentence summary. This will usually become your META DESCRIPTION tag on the syndication service.

News Body. Copy and paste your news body. Be sure to embed a URL after the first or second paragraph, and write in the simple *http://* format (since embedded links may not be retained in syndicated press releases).

URL / Active Link. Make sure that your press release has at least one prominent link to your website, and **make sure it is in the http:// format**. News is especially good at getting Google to index new web pages on your site!

Contact Information. Include a description of your company with a Web link and email address for more information. This is another link-building opportunity.

Tags. Select appropriate tags for keyword / content issues as well as target geographies.

Finally, commit to publishing press releases on your website and using news syndication on a regular, consistent basis. It's better to publish one release per month, consistently, than six releases in one month and nothing for six months. For an online press release template, visit http://jmlinks.com/6r. To see sample press releases on PRWEB as written by the JM Internet Group visit http://jmlinks.com/14c.

WORKSHEETS. For the worksheet, go to https://www.jm-seo.org/workbooks (click on "SEO Fitness 2017," enter the code '2017fitness' to register if you have not already done so), and click on the link to the "press release worksheet."

VIDEO. Watch a quick video tutorial on how to syndicate press releases at http://jmlinks.com/18f.

A Warning about the Penguin Update

Google's latest anti-SEO algorithm update has been called the "Penguin Update." The Penguin Update specifically targets low quality link schemes, meaning many inbound links to your website from low-quality sites that often have the same keyword phrase with a link.

The take-away is to not overdo press release SEO! First, don't issue more than two press releases per month via paid syndication services such as PRWeb.com. Second, to every extent possible, use press releases for "real" news with even the goal of getting "real" people to read them (including journalists) and possibly reach out to your company for more information. Don't issue junk, but then again don't be too modest either.

Post-Penguin the goal is to have a "natural" inbound link footprint consisting of branded, naked, and keyword heavy links. Even a few "click here" links are good to throw into the mix.

» DELIVERABLES: A PRESS RELEASE CALENDAR AND A SAMPLE PRESS RELEASE

The first **DELIVERABLE** for this chapter is your press release calendar. This can be as simple as a Word document or Google document that serves as an "idea list" of when to generate a press release. The goal is to avoid writer's block and get into a rhythm of generating at least two press releases per month. The second **DELIVERABLE** is your first SEO-friendly press release, uploaded to your own site and pushed out via a syndication service such as PRLOG.org or PRWEB.com. Use the "press release worksheet" to guide you to success.

4.3

BLOGGING

Nothing is as easy or as powerful for SEO as blogging! While landing pages reflect your anchor keyword terms, and press releases can build inbound links via syndication, blogging allows you to sculpt content for narrower keyword queries as well as to respond quickly to industry buzz and trends. In addition, frequent blogging - like frequent press releases- sends a powerful signal to Google that your website is "fresh." Every website should have a blog!

Let's get started!

TODO LIST:

 ≫ Why Blog?

 ≫ Make a Blog Calendar

 ≫ Set Up Your Blog for Best SEO

 ≫ Write SEO-friendly Blog Posts

 ≫≫ Deliverables: Blog Calendar and Your First Blog Post

≫ WHY BLOG?

Why Blog? Blogging is one of the most powerful, highest return-on-investment (ROI) activities you can engage in, after you've SEO optimized your home page and your landing pages. Here's why. First, an active blog sends out a "freshness" signal to Google, Bing, and Yahoo saying "I'm alive, I'm alive, I'm alive." You have to look at the world from Google's perspective. Google's goal is to return highly relevant, active websites for any search query. So, if a user searches for a *pizza restaurant in Okmulgee, Oklahoma,*

Google has a set of pizza websites to consider. It will choose the one that has optimized for the keywords "Pizza" and "Okmulgee," plus has active inbound links, plus has many reviews on Google, and – all things being equal – the one with the more active blog. Why? Because Google is concerned that the other pizza restaurant – the one without an active blog – is out of business. If it's June 3, 2017, and the last blog post on Website A was May 3, 2017, and the last blog post on Website B was July 1, 2015, and the last blog post on Website C was… *well Website C doesn't even have a blog…* then Website A is the winner (all things being equal). An active blog with recent blog posts on your keyword themes signals to Google, that you're alive.

Second, after freshness, a blog allows you to write content on micro or long tail search keywords. To use our pizza example, the primary keyword might be "Pizza" or "Pizza Okmulgee," but there may be some searches for "best pizza restaurants in Okmulgee for kids' birthday parties." These are *high value, low volume* searches. A quick blog post on how to select the best pizza restaurant in Okmulgee for kids birthdays is an easy way to get to the top of Google for these micro, or long-tail search phrases. So, an active blog allows you to create a lot of content on lots of varied themes. It costs next to nothing, and can be free advertising on long tail keyword queries. How great is that?

Third, an active blog increases the volume of content on your site. All things being equal the bigger site will win on Google. If, for example, Pizza restaurant A has ten pages, and Pizza restaurant B has one hundred pages, then Pizza restaurant B must be better in Google's eyes (all other factors being equal). Bigger means better; more content means a more serious website. Use the *site: command* plus your domain to check how many pages you have indexed on Google, and then use the Search Tools > Anytime > Past Month drop downs to find out if you have new content that is being indexed by Google. Here's a screenshot:

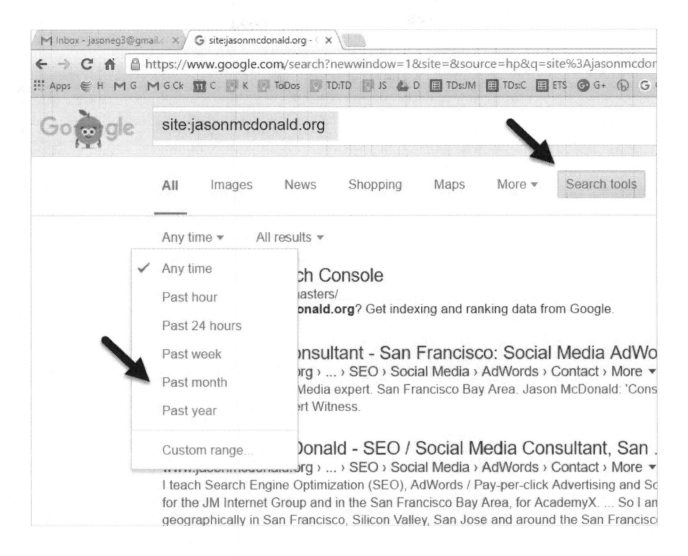

Remember it's *site: **no space** and your domain* as in *site:jasonmcdonald.org* in the Google search bar. To see this in action, visit http://jmlinks.com/14d.

Fourth, a blog allows you to pass link juice up to your landing pages. When you blog on *best pizza restaurant in Okmulgee for kids,* you can link "up" to the landing page for *Pizza* and the landing page for *Okmulgee Pizza* when you use those phrases in your blog, again passing "freshness" and "link juice" up to those landing pages. Finally, a blog (especially long form blog posts) can act as "link bait." When you write an interesting, in-depth blog post on an industry topic, especially trending or puzzling topics, people are likely to find it and link to it, thereby attracting links to your website. In addition, people often share blog articles on social media, helping you both for SEO (by getting social mentions of your URLs and website) and social media marketing (by creating sticky, interesting, sharable content that gets your brand in front of more customers).

In summary, you just gotta blog!

As you begin to blog, remember to stick with your keyword themes. Don't blog on just anything – blog on topics that contain your keywords. Stay on topic.

As an SEO Content strategist, look around your company and identify blog topics as well as other company employees who can contribute to the blog. Unlike press releases, blog posts can be much more informal, opinionated and quick. So whereas you might generate just two press releases per month, set a goal of at least one blog post per week, if not more. I generally recommend two press releases per month and four blog posts per month as a solid website goal. The word *blog*, after all, comes from *web log*, and is meant as a running commentary on what's going on on your website, at your business, and in your industry.

COMMIT TO FOUR BLOG

POSTS PER MONTH

Think of Captain Kirk on the Starship Enterprise: *"Captain's log, Stardate 4.2.51535, Spock and I have beamed down to the planet to investigate. I will check out the beautiful women, and Spock will be taking soil samples."* Kirk logged, and logged, and logged his way across his five year mission, and he was pretty shameless. So don't be shy: blog, blog, blog, blog, blog! If you don't toot your own horn, no one will.

> *You cannot overblog!* As long as your blog content is fresh, original, and keyword-heavy, all blogs posts will help your SEO. The more the merrier!

A Blog Calendar

Depending on your company size, a blog calendar can help you keep track of possible blog topics and themes. You can also assign out the blog posts to different members of your team. Don't try to do all the blogging yourself.

Here is a sample blog calendar for a hypothetical roofing company in Dallas, TX.

Sample Blog Topic:	When To Post:
We complete a roofing job.	Write a blog post about each roofing job, when completed, with information on the city where the job was located, the type of roofing material used, and customer reaction. Goal is to help with geotargeted searches.
Our day-to-day in a host city for a job.	Because geographic search terms are important for a roofing company, create city-specific blog posts such as your favorite "taco joint" in the city, or variances in city roofing codes.
Industry trends and events	Any time there is an industry trend, such as a new roofing material, chime in with an opinion. Ditto for any industry events or events in the Dallas, Texas, area.
New website content	Blog about our website, explaining what new content we are creating and why.
Partnership Announcements	Identify potential blog opportunities with our partners.
Industry Awards or Milestones	Any time we win an industry award or cross a milestone (such as the 1000th follower on Twitter), it's time for a blog post!

You'll see many similarities between successful SEO blogging and SEO press releases. The difference is one of degree: blogging is quicker, more informal, and more a quantity play vs. the more formal, higher quality status of press releases. Commit to writing four blog posts per month, and stick with it.

» Set up Your Blog for Best SEO

The best blog platform by far is WordPress (http://wordpress.org/). Ask you web designer and/or ISP to install WordPress on your site. If you are building a new site, use an ISP like GoDaddy that makes WordPress a "one click" installation. And, if you don't have the budget for WordPress, I recommend Google's blogger platform at http://www.blogger.com/. Regardless of your platform, follow these basic principles for successful SEO blogging:

Host your blog on your own site. Blogging helps with site freshness vis-a-vis Google as well as acts as link bait. So it makes little sense to host your blog on another site. If at all possible, host your blog at your own domain in the position of http://www.company.com/blog.

Check each blog post for good SEO. As you write a blog post, check to make sure that your blogging platform allows for basic "on page" SEO: a keyword heavy TITLE tag, META DESCRIPTION tag, the use of the header family, one image with the alt attribute defined, and keyword-heavy cross-links.

Make sure your blog allows for keyword heavy tagging and cross-indexing. Make sure that your blog allows you to "tag" a post with keywords and that these "tags" act as URL cross-links.

Verify that your blog URLs are keyword heavy. Numeric, parameter-centric URLs are very bad for SEO, so make sure that your blog generates keyword-heavy URLs for each post.

At the home page level, a best practice is to have "one click" links from your home page down to at least three, rotating blog posts. If you are running WordPress, be sure to install the Yoast SEO plug in (https://yoast.com/).

Tag Your Blog in WordPress

Many people do not correctly "tag" each blog post, yet tagging is incredibly important to SEO-friendly blogging! Make sure that your blog tags match your keyword themes, and make sure that when you write a blog post each post gets tagged. One of the better blogs to emulate is by Nolo press (http://blog.nolo.com/). Here's a screenshot of the tags at the bottom of the page for a post on bankruptcy forms:

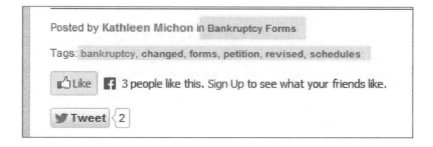

WordPress has two types of tagging: "categories" and "tags." From an SEO perspective, both accomplish the same thing: lumping your posts into SEO-friendly cross-linked URL's. Both are strongly encouraged because both give Google an SEO-friendly URL structure to grab onto. Here's a link to the Nolo blog "Chapter 7" tag: http://jmlinks.com/14j. Notice how the practitioners at Nolo are churning out blog post after blog post on their keyword theme of "Chapter 7," and related keywords! And notice the URL structure itself, which mimics the target keywords and signals to Google that this blog has quite a bit of content on bankruptcy:

http://blog.nolo.com/bankruptcy/tag/chapter-7/

Another example of a good blog can be found on Thomas Upchurch Law. Check out their blog at http://jmlinks.com/14g. Notice how he blogs on his target keyword themes such as "estate planning" and "will contests." To find good blog examples in your own industry, go to Google and do a search for your keywords as in "probate" plus "blog" and then browse the top websites. For an example search, visit http://jmlinks.com/14h.

>> WRITE SEO-FRIENDLY BLOG POSTS

Blogging is a complementary SEO content strategy to your anchor landing pages, your home page, your product pages, and your press releases. Whereas anchor landing pages focus on your evergreen anchor keyword terms, your blog can focus on more keyword specific, timely topics. Blogging is especially useful for posting content that responds to quick industry trends. Here are the steps to writing a good blog post:

1. **Identify the target keywords.** A good blog post is laser focused on a very narrow keyword, so do your keyword research first! Use Ubersuggest.io, Google autocomplete, and the Google Keyword Planner to identify keyword topics and related keywords to your targets.
2. **Follow "on page" SEO best practices.** Make sure that your post follows all of the "on page" rules such as a keyword heavy TITLE, META description, at least one image with an ALT attribute that contains the target keyword, etc.
3. **Consider an action or purpose.** Have a defined action for each blog post, usually by embedding a link from the blog post "up to" one of your defined anchor landing pages. Another use of blog posts such as "Top Ten Things that

Can Go Terribly Wrong at Your Wedding" is link bait; people will link to informative, provocative, shocking blog posts.

4. **Tag your blog post.** Identify keyword themes for your blog that match those of your keyword worksheet and recognize that each blog post is part of a keyword cluster, supporting the entire website's SEO themes.

VIDEO. Watch a video tutorial on SEO-friendly blogging posts at http://jmlinks.com/17t.

For a template on an SEO friendly blog post, visit http://jmlinks.com/14e. For a fun blog topic generator, check out http://jmlinks.com/14f.

» DELIVERABLES: A BLOG CALENDAR AND A SAMPLE BLOG POST

The first **DELIVERABLE** for this chapter is your blog calendar. This can be as simple as a Word document or Google document that serves as an "idea list" of when to generate a blog post. The goal is to avoid writer's block and get into a rhythm of generating at least one blog post per week, if not more. The second **DELIVERABLE** is your first SEO-friendly blog post, uploaded to your own site and tagged with appropriate (keyword) tags. Use the "page tags worksheet" to step through an SEO-friendly blog post from keyword target to final content.

SURVEY OFFER

CLAIM YOUR $10 REBATE OR FREE BOOK! HERE'S HOW –

13. Visit http://jmlinks.com/survey.
14. Take a short, simple survey about the book.
15. Indicate whether you want a $10.00 rebate or a free copy of one of Jason's other books on SEO / Social Media Marketing / Job Search & Career-building.

WE WILL THEN –

- Rebate you the $10.00, or send you a free copy of one of the other books.

~ $10 REBATE OFFER ~

~ LIMITED TO ONE PER CUSTOMER ~

EXPIRES: 3/1/2017

SUBJECT TO CHANGE WITHOUT NOTICE

GOT QUESTIONS? CALL 800-298-4065

5.1

LINK BUILDING

Steps #1 to #3 are "on page" SEO: things you do to your own website. **Step #4** is about **content**: *content marketing, press releases,* and *blogging.* In **Step #5**, we cross the Rubicon, shifting our attention 100% to the actions of others through "off page" SEO. Just as *references* matter to an effective job search, external *links* matter a great deal to effective SEO.

Step #5 in the **Seven Steps to SEO Success**, therefore, is to "go social." Google pays incredible attention to how others talk about your website, whether in the format of inbound HTML *links* or inbound *social mentions.* We'll turn first to **links**, the more traditional of the two, and in the next chapter look directly at **social authority** and **social mentions**. In Chapter 5.3, we'll turn to **reviews**, which for local companies, are a key aspect of "Off Page" SEO.

Remember that a link *from* a directory, blog, web portal, or other industry site *to* your website is counted as a **vote** by Google that your site is important. The *more* links (votes) you have, the *higher* you show on Google search results for your target keywords. But how do you get links? In this Chapter, we outline the basics of effective link building for SEO.

Let's get started!

TODO LIST:

>> Understand Links and Off Page SEO

>> Beware the Penguin

>> Define Your Link Objectives

>> Solicit the Easy Links First

>> Identify Directory, Blog, and Other Link Targets

>> Reverse Engineer Competitors' Links

>> Create Link Bait

>> >> Deliverable: Link Building Worksheet

>> UNDERSTAND LINKS AND OFF PAGE SEO

Google's genius was to be the first search engine that effectively counted links as votes. Prior to Google, search engines basically looked at page content, and it was therefore very difficult to figure out which site was better if the page content itself contained the keywords. Google realized that you could look at how websites linked to other sites, in a kind of grand vote scheme on the Internet.

For example, why do I rank so well for the searches *SEO expert Bay Area*, or *AdWords Expert Witness*? Among the reason is that I have many sites linking to JasonMcDonald.org. BAVC.org, for one, links to my website, JasonMcDonald.org at http://jmlinks.com/6u. In this way, BAVC.org is "voting" that my website is important. Similarly, the Authors Guild (Authorsguild.net) (http://jmlinks.com/18w) also links to me. These "votes" reinforce my On Page SEO and propel me to the top of relevant searches on Google.

Links are Like Votes

In short, a site with more links than its competitors is seen by Google as more important, and ranks higher on Google, all other things being equal. In a bit of circular logic, the site that had more links to it, had higher PageRank (Web Authority) and therefore a link from it was more important. So the more popular a site is, the more link authority it has, and the more links from it matter to Google. (*The popular kids on the Web, just like the popular kids in High School, have all the clout*).

LINKS ARE LIKE VOTES

Think of *links* like *votes in an election*, and you'll understand how it works.

Quantity. How do you win the US Presidential Election? Get more votes. Generally speaking, the candidate who wins the popular vote becomes president. (*OK, not always – but, at least, that's what we tell our kids!*) If two websites are competing, the website with more links must be more important and therefore wins. (**Link quantity**)

Quality. Not all votes are alike, however. The voter must correctly vote for a candidate by marking his or her name correctly on the ballot. (*Think hanging chads in Florida and confusion about voter intent in 2000*). If two websites are competing, the website with more links that contain the keyword target will win (**Link syntax**).

Authority. Not all votes are equal. In the 2016 Presidential election, the votes of people in Michigan counted a lot more than the votes of people in California. Indeed, if you look back to 2000, the votes of the justices on the Supreme Court counted the most, throwing that election to George Bush, even though Al Gore had won the popular vote. (**Link authority** or **PageRank**).

In general, therefore, links are like votes, and you want to secure as many external websites as possible linking to your website. But that's not the whole story: it's more complicated than simple quantity (just like votes in a US Presidential election), so you need a more detailed understanding of how Google counts links.

Let's dive in.

Optimized Link Syntax

An *optimized link*, in contrast, contains the target SEO keyword. For an optimized link with anchor text, visit http://jmlinks.com/14m. Here's a screenshot:

> **Jason McDonald** is one of POMA members' favorite conference presenters. Jason is director of the JM Internet Group, and has been active in Internet marketing since 1994, first in hi-tech for embedded engineers and increasingly in teaching **SEO, social media, and AdWords** to businesspeople and marketers online. Jason also teaches live at Stanford University's Continuing Studies Program as well as in San Francisco. His philosophy is can-do, and hands-on: to position Internet marketing as a marketing challenge – first- and a technical challenge, second. His published books include "*SEO Fitness Workbook*" and "*AdWords Gotchas*," both with many tens of positive review on Amazon. You can find Jason on the Internet by just Googling, 'Jason McDonald' (he's number 1). In his spare time, Jason is devoted to his new Labrador retriever puppy, Buddy.

And here's the HTML code:

```
<a                    href="http://www.jasonmcdonald.org/"
target="_blank">SEO, social media, and AdWords</a>
```

This means that the link itself is telling Google to rank my website for *SEO, Social Media*, and *AdWords*. That's link syntax.

Domain Authority or PageRank

Links from more powerful sites count for more than links from less powerful websites. It stands to reason, for example, that a link from the New York Times (NYTimes.com) is worth more than a link from the Tulsa World (Tulsaworld.com). But the Google algorithm quantifies this difference in authority.

While Google doesn't share its algorithm, third-party tools like AHREFS.com allow you to peek behind the curtain and see the relative Domain Authority of different websites.

For example, NYTimes.com has a Domain Authority of 82, while TulsaWorld.com has a domain authority of 66. Similarly, the *Professionaloutdoormedia.org* has a Domain Authority of 51, and *BAVC.org* has one of 58. In other words, not all links are created or valued equally: a link from the NYTimes.com is worth an incredible amount, and link from Professionaloutdoormedia.org – while valuable – is not worth nearly as much.

If you reverse engineer this, you'll realize that not only do you want to solicit inbound links to your website, you want them:

1. in high **quantity** (more is better);
2. with the **right syntax** (try to get your keywords in the link text itself, rather than just an http:// link or a "click here" link); and
3. from **high Domain Authority** websites (NYTimes.com is worth more than TulsaWorld.com), as well as from sites that are **relevant to your industry** (a link from Brahman.org is worth more to a Brahman cattle ranch website than a link from Pizzaexpo.com.

Link Summary: The Trifecta

In summary, **links** are like **votes**, and you want **quantity**, **quality**, and **authority**. (**Note**: Google does not share much detail about its algorithm, so for a list of tools, go to the dashboard at http://jmlinks.com/seodash and click on the link section). As you solicit links from other websites, remember, however, that you won't always get a *trifecta* or perfect *quantity*, *quality*, and *authority* from a link, so get what you can.

A Word about NoFollow

At a technical level, the `rel="nofollow"` attribute tells Google to ignore a link; these types of links are devalued by Google. So if you see *nofollow* in the HTML source code it's a sign that given link is not as valuable. Here's a screenshot of the Pokemon page on Wikepedia with an outbound link to the official Pokemon website:

External links

- Official Japanese website of *Pokémon* (Japanese)
- Official US website of *Pokémon*
- Official UK website of *Pokémon*

And here's the HTML source code showing the link, including the *nofollow* attribute, therefore nullifying the link:

```
<a         rel="nofollow"         class="external         text"
href="http://www.pokemon.com/">Official US website of
<i>Pokémon</i></a>
```

You can see it at http://jmlinks.com/6w. What this means is that the link FROM Wikipedia TO pokemon.com does NOT help its SEO because the nofollow attribute tells Google NOT to count the link as a vote. Commonly, as you look for links to get to your website, be sure to look at the source code and if you see the *nofollow* attribute then these links are not valuable. The most common are links from blog comments, links from social media site profiles, links from some associations or directories.

Note: a link that does NOT contain the *nofollow* attribute is commonly referred to as a *dofollow* link, although there isn't technically a *dofollow* attribute.

Don't freak out, however, and don't overthink it. You don't have to be an HTML source code genius to understand links! Just realize that, generally speaking, links in comments on blogs are all *nofollow*. Craig's list, Wikipedia, and many directory links are also *nofollow*. Press release links are commonly *nofollow* too. These links are not as valuable as links that do not have the *nofollow* attribute (called *dofollow* links in SEO lingo).

However… in SEO there's always another twist of the screw…

Do Nofollow Links Matter?

The first take-away is that *nofollow* links do *not* help SEO. This is the official Google position and commonly held position in the SEO community. However (*there's always a however in SEO*), my opinion is that *nofollow* links actually *do* count, and can help your SEO. Think of links like a stock portfolio: you want diversity in your links – some *nofollow*, some *dofollow*, some in the HTTP format, some in your brand name, and some in your keyword syntax. *Nofollow* links are like "penny stocks" – one-by-one, not very valuable but in totality, they can indeed be valuable.

Google, in short, probably devalues the weight of *nofollow* links to the tune of 90% or 95%, but they still seem to carry some weight. No one knows for certain but because

Google has terrified so many sites into making blank *nofollows* across all outbound links, Google has created a problem for itself. For many smaller sites (competing for many narrow keywords), there aren't many links that differentiate site #1 from site #2. This is often the case for many small businesses. You might have ten links, and your competitor might have seven. And if all (or most) of these links are nofollows, then Google still has to decide. Presto! *Nofollow* links suddenly count.

Just Get Links

Now, before your head is swimming with all this technical mumbo-jumbo: just remember to **get links**. Ask customers, suppliers, and other business contacts whom you know to add a link FROM their website TO your website. It can be as simple as asking the janitorial company that cleans your office, or the pizza company that delivers your office pizza, to go on their website and add a link FROM their site TO your site. Or, to ask a customer who has a blog to write a product review about her experience, and have her include a link in that blog post FROM her blog TO your website. Or, ask Mom, Dad, Uncle Jay, your best friend... anyone who has a blog to write up an article about you, and link TO your website.

Register for professional associations that include links to your website. Set up your social profiles on Twitter, Facebook, Google+ and other sites. Ask everyone you know who has a website to write something about your company and link over to it.

Just get links!

Just like in real-world elections, the most important part of successful link building is sheer **quantity**. Politicians don't always sweat the small stuff; they kiss a lot of babies, and shake a lot of hands in their quest for high quality votes. So should you in your quest for links!

POLITICIANS KISS BABIES

SEOS ASK FOR LINKS

For a nice online tutorial on links and SEO, check out the MOZ guide at http://jmlinks.com/14n.

» BEWARE THE PENGUIN

Google's "Penguin" update, launched in April 2012, is an on-going algorithm attack against artificial link-building. While officially Google says that you should NEVER "build links" but rather just wait "passively" for links to come to your site, a passive strategy will get you nowhere.

You can, must, and should "build links."

However, you have to be aware of Penguin, and solicit links in a smart fashion. First, let's consider what Penguin penalizes, and then let's turn to the "big picture" of link-building, post-Penguin.

First, Penguin penalizes a large quantity of in-bound links from "low quality" websites as well as "overoptimized links." "Low quality" websites are generally artificial blogs – blogs that are poorly written, contain non-related content, and are clearly created "for search engines" and not for people. A good example of this scenario is Indian-based SEO companies that built thousands upon thousands of blogs (called a blog network), and then (for money) will link back to your site around a target keyword phrase such as *Miami divorce attorney*, or *organic baby food*. It is easy for Google to detect this chicanery and penalize sites with this sort of a link footprint.

In fact, if you are solicited by SEO companies offering link schemes that directly involve posting links to your website on low quality blogs or low quality directories, do **NOT** fall for these schemes! They will hurt you much more than help you.

What are Overoptimized Links?

"Overoptimized" links are links from other websites to your website that all include the same keyword phrase over and over. A "divorce attorney," for example, might create / pay for / solicit links from blogs all around the exact phrase "divorce attorney." He would end up with, for example, 1000 blogs all linking back to his website, all having the format of:

bla, bla, bla, bla, bla divorce attorney (linking to: http://www.divorceattorneywebsite.com) bla bla bla bla bla bla bla

Now, to have 1000 links all exactly alike, all linking back to the same website is "unnatural," isn't it? So what Penguin did was look at the "link footprint" of websites and identify "unnatural" link footprints. It then penalizes these sites by taking them off of Google or harshly pushing them from Page 1 to Page 101.

Penguin looks for "unnatural" link profiles: many links from low quality blogs or directories as well as many optimized links. You can use the Remove 'em tool at http://jmlinks.com/6x to check your own link footprint.

Link Diversity

Second, when building links post-Penguin, you should a) never solicit links from low quality blogs and/or easy, free directories, and certainly not get links from sites the blatantly advertise "links for sale," and b) pay attention to the (over)optimization of your link structure. A good general rule of thumb is 1/3 *http://* links, 1/3 *branded* links (links to your company name), and 1/3 *optimized* links. In HTML code these are written as:

```
Check out Jason McDonald's SEO consulting website at
https://www.jasonmcdonald.org/ (naked or http link).

Check out <a href=http://www.jasonmcdonald.org/>Jason
McDonald's</a> SEO consulting website. (branded link)

Check out Jason McDonald, an amazing <a
href=http://www.jasonmcdonald.org/>SEO consultant</a> in
San Francisco. (optimized link)
```

Link diversity means having people link to you in different formats, and to get links from a variety of sources: trade associations, blogs, directories, non-profits, etc.

Fortunately, for most companies, too many links and *too many* overoptimized links are the least of their problems; most companies just have *too few* links. But, that said, if you engage in serious link-building, you must "beware the Penguin" and build a "natural" yet robust inbound link profile. Build links at your own risk!

Outbound Links from Your Website

Finally, Penguin penalizes websites that are "too perfect." Pre-Penguin, many SEO experts would advise you never to link out FROM your website TO other websites. This advice is no longer correct; a website that has zero outbound links looks suspicious to Google. Similarly, many websites would use the *nofollow* attribute on all outbound links, or to "sculpt" links internally. After Penguin, this kind of behavior is a dead giveaway that you are attempting to manipulate Google. So, don't be "too perfect:"

> Do not refuse to link outbound to other websites because a website with zero outbound links looks suspicious to Google.
>
> Do not "nofollow" all your links to other websites, as the use of "nofollow" on all outbound links can also look suspicious to Google.
>
> Do not "nofollow" certain internal links in an attempt to link sculpt, as this also looks suspicious to Google.

Therefore, post-Penguin, I advise you to strategically link out to highly reputable websites in your industry. A breeder of Brahman cattle, for example, should link out to sites like the National Brahman Association (brahman.org) as well as other websites in the cattle industry. A San Francisco attorney might link to the city of San Francisco (SFgov.org). The objective is to convince Google that you are a good "Net citizen," and you are linking *out* as well as receiving links *in*. Just keep your outbound links to a minimum, and make sure that they are to highly reputable sites in your own industry.

Google's Hypocrisy

As we conclude this explanation of what links are, why they matter, and the basic ideas on how to build links *post-Penguin,* let me stop for a moment and talk about Google's hypocrisy. Google famously had the phrase "Don't be evil" as their corporate motto, which besides being pretentious, has probably turned out to be yet another empty platitude by yet another big corporation. Google, like all big corporations, keeps its eyes on profits, and has a very effective corporate marketing machine working hard to create a brand image of efficiency and honesty. Google isn't any better, or any worse, than any other big corporation.

In terms of links, the official propaganda of Google is that no one should ever build links. (Read it at http://jmlinks.com/14r). In Google's opinion, we should all just passively wait until links "spontaneously" emerge on the Web, and then Google will "objectively" evaluate the link footprint of competing websites and choose the "best" website to place at the top of its results.

I'm sorry to destroy your illusions, but if you've read this far in this book, you should realize, by now, that the idea that Google results are "objective" is pretty ridiculous. It's a competitive war between companies to get to the top, and in any serious keyword competition, everyone is working very hard to "manipulate" Google. Your competitors (at least the smart ones) are building links, and you pretty much have to, too, even though Google's official public line is that you should NEVER solicit links.

Everyone, quite simply, has to violate the rules without any clear guidance as to what the "real" rules are. Google simply looks the other way, and occasionally smacks down a vendor or two when it gets out of hand. You can either be 100% compliant with Google's policy on links (*and end up spending a fortune on AdWords*), or you can violate Google's policy and succeed.

It gets worse. Google even encourages companies to "turn in" competitors that are violating its policies. Watch an official video on this at http://jmlinks.com/14t. You can even "turn in" a competitor via the official Google webspam form at http://jmlinks.com/14u. Here's a screenshot:

Google

Search Console

Help us maintain the quality of Google search results.

We work hard to return the most relevant results for every search we
have users' best interests at heart. Some site owners attempt to "buy

Google uses a number of methods to detect paid links, including alg
submissions, and we'll use your data to improve our algorithmic dete

Report paid links

Website selling links:

Website buying links:

Nefariously, the effect of all these activities is to encourage users to turn in other users as well as what to create "negative SEO" when one competitor "fakes" noncompliance by another competitor (and turns them in) to destroy their website performance. It's a mess, and far, far from "don't be evil" in terms of its impact. Yet Google, happily making millions, doesn't seem very concerned about the devastating impact its policies have on websites, or on the "unintended consequences" of its policies.

Now, I'm not saying go 100% to the dark side via black hat SEO and build or buy fake links. And I'm not saying I have a solution for how this could be done differently. I'm not Google, and I don't have a zillion dollar budget to figure out a solution. *It's Google's world; we just live in it*. But what I am saying is put your best foot forward, solicit real links from real websites, and you'll go a long way towards succeeding. But don't publicly announce what you're doing, and don't wave a red flag under Google's nose.

Similarly, with respect to the *nofollow* attribute in Web links, Google publicly says that it nullifies the value of all links, but in my experience, this isn't exactly true. Some *nofollow* links do seem to help. And, even more ominously, there are many, many examples of websites that are heavily violating Google's policies on links, and doing very, very well. Enforcement of any rules is sporadic at best, and Google takes periodic action against high profile violators to "frighten" the SEO community into compliance. See, for example, the "Rap Genius" incident in which Google made an "example" of Rap Genius as a site that had gone "too far" in soliciting links at http://jmlinks.com/14s. There are many, many sites that are violating Google's policies just as badly, but Rap Genius was singled out, and made an example.

Be Skeptical. Experiment and Do What Works

The bottom line is that you should be skeptical about what Google says are the rules, and what the rules are. You should be skeptical about what you read in the blogosphere about these policies. And you should be silent when, and if, your website is doing well in terms of SEO for fear that a competitor will turn you into Google. You should not get greedy and "go too far." The art of SEO is figuring out what actually works despite what Google says, despite what you read, and staying pretty silent about it. Just as you might drive on Highway 101 in California – speed, but don't be the fastest car on the freeway. As for the posted speed limit, it's not the "real" limit, but who knows what the "real" limit is? You certainly can't ask the Highway Patrol.

So, now that we've taken a little side journey into Google's misleading and contradictory policies on links, let's return to some relatively safe tactics to build links to your own website (at your own risk, of course).

» DEFINE YOUR LINK OBJECTIVES

Now that you know the game – that *links are like votes*, it's time to define your objectives. We'll assume you've SEO optimized your home page, landing pages, keyword footer, and that you've begun to blog and issue press releases. Those tasks are done, or underway. In terms of links, therefore:

- Links are like votes, i.e. quantity.
  - **Objective**: *get people to link to you.*

- Link syntax matters, i.e. quality. It matters whether links are around your keyword phrases and/or come from content that talks about your keyword themes.
  - o **Objective**: *get links that contain your keyword phrases.*
- Link PageRank or Web Authority matters, i.e. authority. Some sites (e.g., NYTimes.com) or more authoritative than others (e.g., TulsaWorld.com).
  - o **Objective**: get authoritative sites to link to you.
- Link Footprint matters, meaning you want a "natural" footprint of about 1/3 naked http links, 1/3 branded links, and 1/3 optimized links from quality websites.
  - o **Objective**: increase inbound links to your website but do so in a "natural" way in terms of the footprint.

In terms of authority, also realize that in any given industry, certain industry hubs are considered very authoritative. If you are selling Brahman cattle, for example, http://www.brahman.org/, the website of the American Brahman Breeders Association is the most authoritative website for the keyword Brahman cattle. Your **objective** here is to identify the most authoritative websites in your industry and get them to link to you.

Don't Get Discouraged

Now that you know the link game, don't get discouraged. People commonly think, "Dratz, no one will link to us... we are so boring... or our industry is so dumb that no one will link to anyone." However, you don't have to run faster than your buddy, just faster than the bear! You're not running for President of the United States, it's more likely that you're running for school board in Okmulgee, Oklahoma, an election decided by tens or hundreds of votes. Your competitor faces the same challenges as you, so if you just pro-actively solicit links – even just a few links – you'll usually win.

He might have two links to his website, and you'll have three. You win.

He might have ten links to his website, and you'll have twelve. You win.

Let's turn, now, to **link-building**: systematic strategies for getting other websites to link to your website for SEO. (For an in-depth list of ideas to help you brainstorm your link-building tactics, check out the PointBlankSEO guide at *http://jmlinks.com/14p*).

» SOLICIT THE EASY LINKS FIRST

Your **ecosystem partners**, i.e. those companies you do business with on a regular basis, are your easiest link targets. If you attend an industry trade show as an exhibitor, for example, ask for a link back to your company website from the trade show website. If you buy a lot of stuff from a supplier, require a link back to your company website from their website as a condition of doing business. If you sponsor a local charity like the *Breast Cancer Walk Pittsburgh*, ask for a link back to your company website from the charity website. If your boss teaches a class at the local university, help him set up a link from his or her profile page back to your company website. If anyone in your company gets interviewed or is able to write a guest blog post on another website, make sure that they get a link back in their author profile!

You get the idea: create a **culture of link solicitation** in your organization, so that on a day-in and day-out level everyone in your company is soliciting links, and (over time) getting them.

Don't forget your **social media profile** links! If local search is important to you, make sure that your company is included in Google+ Local, Yelp, Citysearch and other local listing sites. Be sure to set up a Twitter, Google+, Facebook and other social media profiles for your companies and include links in those profiles. Don't forget your **directory links**! If your industry has serious, quality, industry-specific directories, make sure you are included in those directory listings with links.

VIDEO. Watch a video tutorial on easy link-building tactics at http://jmlinks.com/17w.

Your first **TODO** is to open up the "link building worksheet," and fill out the easy link target section. For the worksheet, go to https://www.jm-seo.org/workbooks (click on "SEO Fitness 2017," enter the code '2017fitness' to register if you have not already done so), and click on the link to the "link building worksheet."

» IDENTIFY DIRECTORY, BLOG, AND OTHER LINK TARGETS

Quality directories, blogs, and other websites found on Google make great link targets. How do you find them? For **directories**, do a Google search for keywords such as "AddURL + Your Keywords," "Directory + Your Keywords," and/or "Catalog + Your

Keywords." As you browse these sites, make note of their **Web Authority** (*use MOZ.com or AHREFS.com, and the Domain Authority metric*) and **keyword themes** that align with your own target keywords. Use the Solo SEO link search tool (*http://jmlinks.com/14q*) for a quick and easy way to look for possible link targets.

A marriage counselor in Bethesda, Maryland, for example, might search Google for:

> *marriage counselor directory (view this search at http://jmlinks.com/6y)*
>
> *directory of therapists*
>
> *relationship therapist directory*
>
> *directory Maryland businesses*
>
> *directory woman-owned businesses*

Her goals are to a) identify quality directories that have *dofollow* outbound links, b) figure out how much it costs and/or what are the procedures to be listed, and c) acquire those directory links. **Remember**: if it's absolutely easy to get in, every SEO will do it and the directory will be low quality or contaminated. **You want serious directories that either cost money and/or have real qualifications to be included.** Quality is important!

Identify Relevant Blogs

To find **blogs**, type your target keywords plus the word "blog" into the Google search box. For example, our marriage therapist might type in "marriage therapy blog" at http://jmlinks.com/19h. IceRocket at http://www.icerocket.com/ is a specialized search engine just to find blogs. You're looking for blogs that will allow a guest post and/or blogs that are interested in your keywords. Remember to also pro-actively ask customers if they have a blog, and if they do, solicit them to write something about your company, product or service. Then you have to devise an idea / solicitation that they'd like to include on their blog, plus include a link back to your website.

A common tactic is to give out product samples, for free, in exchange for a product review and link back on the blog. (Again, with an eye to Google's sensitivity about links, don't "overdo" this – find high quality, legitimate bloggers, and don't publicly announce your product-review-link program!). Do NOT go to a public blog exchange and buy links – that's way too obvious, and too dangerous!

Complementary Competitors

Finally, do searches for your major keyword phrases. As you search, segregate your **direct competitors** (sites so similar to your own that there is no way that they would link to you) from your **complementary competitors**. These are sites like blogs, personal websites, portals, directories, Wiki entries and the like that "show up" on your searches but may have a complementary reason to link to you. A wedding photographer, for example, might search for not only directories of wedding suppliers but also florists, priests, caterers, bakers, and facilities that would likely exchange links due to the complementary nature of their businesses.

Sponsor Non-Profits and Include Links

Another great tactic is non-profit link-building. Solicit non-profit links: identify relevant non-profits, and pay them as a "sponsor" with a link from their website to your own. As with all link-building tactics, do not overdo this.

A good way to do this is to search Google using the site: command, as in:

site:*.org "your keywords"

For example: site:*org "organic food" (http://jmlinks.com/7d).

For example: site:*.org "organic food" "link to your website" (http://jmlinks.com/7e).

You thus identify non-profits in your keyword community, and can even drill down to those that allow paying sponsors to link back to their website. Voila: a link-building strategy based on helping non-profits!

VIDEO. Watch a video tutorial on how to identify nonprofits for link-building at http://jmlinks.com/18e.

Todo for Link-Building

Your second **TODO** is to fill out the section of the "link building worksheet" focusing on blogs, portals, and directories. For the worksheet, go to https://www.jm-seo.org/workbooks (click on "SEO Fitness 2017," and enter the code 'fitness' to register if you have not already done so), and click on the link to the "link building worksheet." I highly recommend the PointBlankSEO link-building guide at *http://jmlinks.com/14p* as you begin brainstorming your link strategy.

≫ REVERSE ENGINEER COMPETITORS' LINKS

Wouldn't it be wonderful to be able to "reverse engineer" who links to your competitors, and then solicit links from those websites? You can easily do this.

Many free fabulous tools exist to "reverse engineer" inbound links of competitors. Your objective is to identify complementary websites that link to a competitor but who may also be willing to link to you. Type each competitor's home page URL into these tools, and then surf to the appropriate websites, making note of the PageRank (domain authority), content, and contact information for your "Link Building" target list. Here are my three favorites:

Open Site Explorer by Moz (https://moz.com/researchtools/ose/). Type your competitor's home page into this tool, or the URL of a highly ranked site on Google. Browse to see who is linking to your competitors.

Ahrefs (http://ahrefs.com/). Similar to Open Site Explorer, this free tool allows you to input a competitor URL and reverse engineer who is linking to that competitor.

Open Link Profiler (http://www.openlinkprofiler.org/**).** This tool tracks new links to your website (or to competitors), and requires no registration and no payment. It's totally free!

Here's a screenshot of Open Site Explorer's analysis of http://www.progressive.com/ showing that that site has over 3900 linking domains totaling to over 34,000 inbound links. No wonder *progressive.com* dominates searches for insurance!

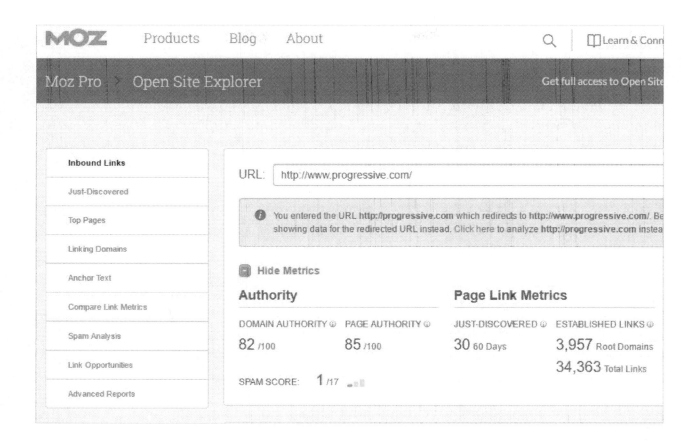

VIDEO. Watch a video on how to use the AHREFS tool and other link discovery tools to "reverse engineer" competitors at http://jmlinks.com/18d.

At the end of this process, you should have a defined list of "link targets" sorted by PageRank (Domain Authority) and their keyword themes with your "keyword community." Your third **TODO** is to take this list, and then go one by one through the results, soliciting links from the various targets. If summer is here, link solicitation is a great task for a cheap intern! Or, go to a site like Fiverr.com (http://www.fiverr.com/) and identify a cheap outsourced worker to do the "grunt" work of your link solicitation system.

≫ CREATE LINK BAIT

Link bait takes link building to the next level. Link bait is the art of creating content that is so compelling that people will *spontaneously* link to it, without you even having to ask. Let's run through some common link-bait ideas.

Ego Bait

Have a customer of the month contest (if your customers have websites), have a supplier of the month award (if your suppliers have websites). Email, call, and even give gifts to blogs, portals, and other content sites that might be willing to cover you and your company. In link building, remember you are dealing with other people, so look at the situation from their perspective: what's in it for them? If you "feature" them with an award, they'll often spontaneously link to you – plus your "award contest" can get press, publicity, and links.

Product Sample Bait

Give away free samples of your product only to people who have a blog, and/or are willing to share your site on social media. Ask them to write honest product reviews, and require a link back in the blog article.

Scholarship Bait

Identify a noble cause (preferably relating to your keyword targets), and create a scholarship program for deserving students. Next, require an essay as part of the application (which will be great content for your blog, and ego bait). Then, identify relevant colleges and solicit them to link "out" to your scholarship. It's win win: the student gets a scholarship, and you get links from quality .edu domains to your website.

Ultimate Guide Bait

Your **blog** can be great link bait. Write the definitive article on "top ten new technologies" for your industry, write a provocative blot post on why "such-and-such" is a "terrible" idea to stir controversy, share an emotional story. Blog posts that are informative, controversial, or emotional tend to get shared, and linked to, the most.

Here's a great example. PointBlank SEO has written the "definitive guide" to Link Building (which is, in and of itself, link bait) at http://jmlinks.com/7b.

Badge Bait

Consider creating **badges**: customer of the month, best tool for such-and-such, partner companies, verification of a certification test, and so on and so forth.

Have you ever noticed how many Yelp results show up high on Google search? Have you ever thought of how many companies have Yelp badges on their websites, with links up to their Yelp listings? Consider being the "Yelp" of your industry via badges. Here's a screenshot giving an inside look at how Yelp promotes its link juice via badges:

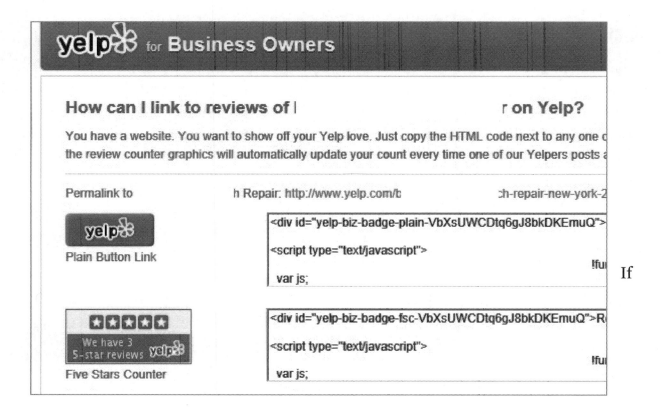

You can view the Yelp badge system at http://jmlinks.com/7f. Note: if you use "badge bait," be Penguin-aware. Make sure to **vary the inbound link text** and structure across your badges so as to not trigger a Penguin penalty. For example, the ALT image attribute for some badges would have keyword No. 1, others keyword No. 1, others just your company name, etc.

Widget Bait

If you have a programming budget, create **widgets** such as BMI calculator, the real-time price of gold, a reverse mortgage calculator. Any sort of free tool or widget that is relevant to your industry can be link bait to bring in links in a spontaneous way. Monex, a company that sells gold, silver, and platinum bullion, for example, has an example of "widget bait" at http://jmlinks.com/7c. **Infographics** are another way to get links: create an informative, humorous, outrageous or shocking infographic and let the links roll in!

Your fourth **TODO** is to have a company meeting and brainstorm possibilities for link bait. If so, create a step-by-step plan to implement your link bait strategy.

▶▶ DELIVERABLE: A COMPLETED LINK-BUILDING WORKSHEET

The **DELIVERABLE** for this chapter is a completed link-building worksheet. For the worksheet, go to https://www.jm-seo.org/workbook (click on "SEO Fitness 2017," and enter the code '2017fitness' to register if you have not already done so), and click on the link to the "link-building worksheet." (For an in-depth list of ideas to help you brainstorm your link-building strategies, check out the PointBlankSEO guide at *http://jmlinks.com/14p*).

SURVEY OFFER

CLAIM YOUR $10 REBATE OR FREE BOOK! HERE'S HOW –

16. Visit http://jmlinks.com/survey.
17. Take a short, simple survey about the book.
18. Indicate whether you want a $10.00 rebate or a free copy of one of Jason's other books on SEO / Social Media Marketing / Job Search & Career-building.

WE WILL THEN –

- Rebate you the $10.00, or send you a free copy of one of the other books.

~ $10 REBATE OFFER ~

~ LIMITED TO ONE PER CUSTOMER ~

EXPIRES: 3/1/2017

SUBJECT TO CHANGE WITHOUT NOTICE

GOT QUESTIONS? CALL 800-298-4065

5.2
SOCIAL MEDIA

A topic unto itself, Social Media has many SEO implications. **Social mentions** - that is the sharing of your website links on sites like Twitter, Google+, Facebook and more - is a new kind of **link building**. Having robust **social profiles** (like an active *Twitter feed* or active *Google+ account*) signals Google and its search algorithm that your company is active and important. This is called **social authority**. Indeed, Google+ presents unique SEO opportunities, particularly in the area of having a robust Google+ corporate profile with many local reviews, as we shall discuss in Chapter 5.3 In addition, Google's partnership with Twitter is a clear sign that having a robust Twitter profile and having your links "tweeted" is now a must-do.

SEO is going social, so in this chapter, we explore the brave new world of **Social Media SEO**.

Let's get started!

TODO LIST:

» Understand Social Media SEO

» Get Social Mentions!

» Set up Robust Social Profiles

» Get Google+: Google's Favored Social Network

»» Deliverable: A Completed Social Media SEO Worksheet

» UNDERSTAND SOCIAL MEDIA SEO

Links, as we have seen, count as **votes** in SEO. Google clearly rewards sites that have many keyword-relevant links (especially those from high authority websites), with higher positions on Google search results. Social Media in a sense builds on this network of link authority. How so? While Google has not publicly clarified how it uses what are called *social signals* in SEO, we can postulate some logical patterns of how Google might interpret social signals.

> *If Website A has its URL "Tweeted" and Website B does not, then Website A must be more important.*
>
> *If blog post A on trending topic #1 has 12 tweets of its URL, and blog post B on trending topic #1 has 35 tweets of its URL, then blog post B must be more relevant for the corresponding Google search query.*
>
> *If Website A has 20,000 followers on Twitter, and Website B has only 100, then Website A must be more important.*
>
> *In a nutshell, having your URL's tweeted, shared on LinkedIn or Facebook, or mentioned on Google+ is a form of link-building.*

Evidence that this occurs is visible in how Google quickly figures out trending news. It's common knowledge that the first place people go to for breaking news is Twitter, and accordingly, a quick Google search of a trending topic (try searching Google, for example, for "The Kardashians," or "Donald Trump," or "iPhone Games") and you'll often find new and fresh content that is being shared heavily on Twitter. In addition, Google has a formal partnership of Twitter in which Google gets first crack at the Twitter "firehose" of breaking news. It stands to reason, therefore, that having your URLs shared on Twitter might help them for SEO purposes.

How does social media impact SEO?

First and foremost, sites that enjoy **inbound links via social mentions of URLs** from social sites like Twitter, Google+, or even Facebook are clearly topical and relevant to Google. A simple *site:twitter.com* search on Google reveals over one billion indexed Tweets, and a simple *site:facebook.com* search on Google reveals over six billion indexed Facebook posts.

Google clearly pays attention to the social sharing of links!

SOCIAL SHARES ARE THE

NEW LINK-BUILDING!

Second, robust and active **social profiles** are another obvious clue to Google of your website's relevance. Many sites link out to their Yelp account, Google+ profile, Twitter account, Facebook page, LinkedIn page, etc., and those social sites can be indexed by Google. Google can clearly "see" how active your company is on social media, how many "followers" you have, and whether those followers, in turn are active and/or important. Most importantly, Google can "count" your "reviews" on Google+, Yelp, YellowPages and other local review sites.

(**Note**: we discuss the impact of reviews in the next Chapter, 5.3 on "Local SEO").

It stands to reason that having an active social media footprint, with active posts, many engaged followers, and many reviews is a new signal to Google about your website's relevance. Indeed, much of this is keyword centric, another reason why knowing your keywords is paramount to SEO success!

Third, social search has made the Web more **human**. Whereas in the past, the creators of Web content were relatively invisible, new ways of communicating "microdata" can tell Google how many reviews your site has, who the content author is, and whether this author has an active, engaged follower community or not. Realizing that SEO is now a **social game** positions your company for not just the present but the future of SEO success on Google.

Note: this Chapter focuses on using social media for SEO purposes. For social media marketing in its own right, please see my *Social Media Marketing Workbook* available on Amazon at http://jmlinks.com/smm.

To be clear, remember that "traditional links" remain far, far more important than social shares to this day: so if you have to choose between a "traditional link" (e.g., from a blog post) and a "social share" (e.g., the Tweeting of your URL), choose the former. **Links still remain the dominant currency of SEO.**

» GET SOCIAL MENTIONS!

Getting **social mentions** of your URLs is a lot like traditional link building. First, look for easy social mention targets. Ask customers, suppliers, and ecosystem partners to tweet your URLs, share your company's blog posts on Facebook, and to "+1" your URLs on Google and to "like" them on Facebook. Second, "reverse engineer" competitors or use common Google and social media searches to find social media sharers who might be interested in your content.

Get Tweeted

For example, to find people Tweeting on your keywords, go to Twitter advanced search at http://jmlinks.com/14w, type in your competitor names or your keywords and look for Tweeters who have a) many followers, and b) tweet on your keyword themes. Then reach out to them and encourage them to tweet your latest blog post, press release, or informative new widget. Here's a screenshot showing a search for tweets on "organic food":

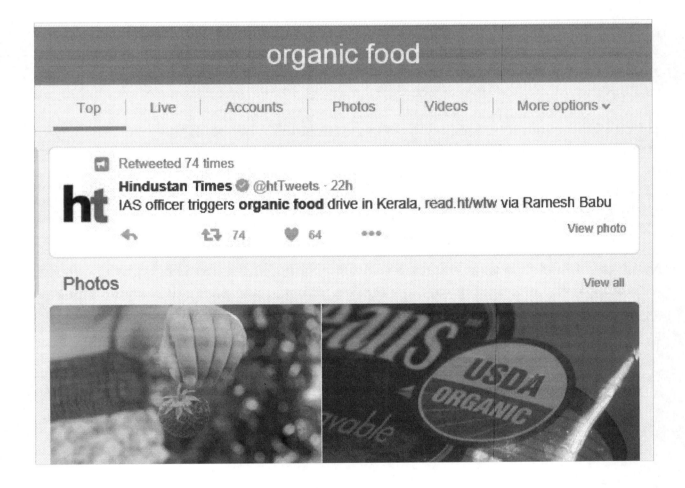

Similarly, you can use Buzzsumo (http://www.buzzsumo.com) to identify social shares of your keywords. Here's a screenshot:

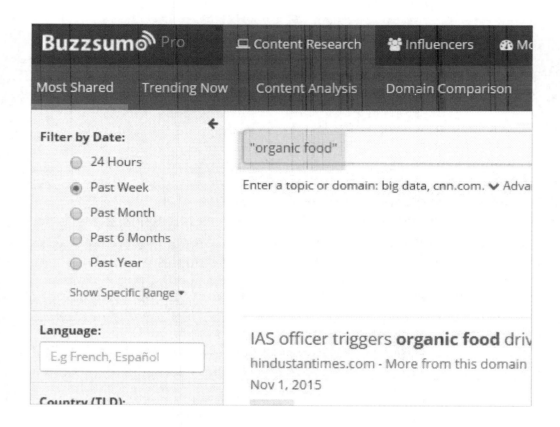

If you've written a blog post on a trending topic, consider advertising on Twitter, Google+, Facebook and/or LinkedIn to get it "picked up" while still timely, thereby encouraging more "free" shares of your URL.

> **VIDEO.** Watch a video tutorial on how to get "social mentions" at http://jmlinks.com/17v.

Google is another great way to search other social media sites for heavy sharers. Try Google searches like *site:facebook.com {your keywords}*, *site:linkedin.com {your keywords}*, *site:pinterest.com {your keywords}*, etc. to identify site-specific individuals who are good targets to share your own content. You can try a sample search at http://jmlinks.com/7h.

VIDEO. Watch a video tutorial on how to use the site: command to identify social sharers at http://jmlinks.com/16g.

Reach out to Bloggers

Don't forget blogs! Go to Google, type in your keywords plus the word "blog" and look for relevant blogs. Social Mention (http://www.socialmention.com) is another search engine that focuses specifically on blogs, as does IceRocket (http://www.icerocket.com/).

As you reach out for links and social mentions, focus on win-win opportunities. For example, if you sell products send out product samples to key bloggers, Tweeters, and Google+'rs and ask them for honest product reviews, "tweets" of your URls, and "shares" of your links on Facebook or Google+, in exchange for samples.

(Remember, however, that – technically speaking – any type of link-building outreach is a violation of Google terms of service so be judicious, and act at your own risk.)

Your first **TODO** is to open the "Social Media SEO worksheet," and complete the section entitled "social sharers." For the worksheet, go to https://www.jm-seo.org/workbooks/ (click on "SEO Fitness 2017," and enter the code '2017fitness' to register if you have not already done so), and click on the link to the "Social Media SEO worksheet."

» SET UP ROBUST SOCIAL PROFILES

It's a no-brainer that Google looks for companies with robust social pages. Given two companies competing for a top position on Google, one with thousands of people circling its Google+ corporate page, and another without a Google+ corporate page at all, to whom do you think Google is going to give top placement? This same fact probably goes for other social networks as well, especially ones like Twitter, Facebook, LinkedIn, YouTube, or Pinterest that are open to the Google crawler at least the account level. (Facebook is closed to Google at the so-called "registration wall.")

For each social media network, be sure to fill out your company pages with relevant keywords and cross-link from each social profile to your website. Leaving aside Google+, here are the most important for most companies with links to their business help guides (if available):

Facebook (https://www.facebook.com/business)

Twitter (https://business.twitter.com/)

LinkedIn (http://jmlinks.com/14x)

YouTube (http://jmlinks.com/7j)

Pinterest (http://business.pinterest.com/)

Once you set up a business page, be sure to populate your company description with your relevant keywords and cross-link it back to your website. Be sure to also link from your home page to your social network pages to make it easy for Google to see which website corresponds to which social network. All of the networks have easy to use badges that enable these important **cross links**; just look for badges in the relevant business help center as listed above. Be sure to be consistent about your physical address, telephone number, and website address.

Posting SEO-friendly Content

Finally, as you post content to a social network, keep your keywords in minds, grow your fan base, and encourage interactivity between you and your fans. Social media is a two-for-one benefit: first, the *direct* benefit from the social media platform itself as you engage with users, and second, the *indirect* benefit as Google "observes" how popular you are and feeds that data into its SEO algorithm.

Your second **TODO** is to open up the "Social Media SEO worksheet" and complete the section "Social Media Profiles." For the worksheet, go to https://www.jm-seo.org/workbooks (click on "SEO Fitness 2017," and enter the code '2017fitness' to register if you have not already done so), and click on the link to the "Social Media SEO worksheet."

» GET GOOGLE+: GOOGLE'S FAVORED SOCIAL NETWORK

Guess who owns Google+? **Google**! Guess who owns search: **Google**!

Think about what that **cross-ownership** means for SEO. Google wants Google+ to succeed, and it "rewards" companies that participate in Google+ with better SEO performance. This is especially true with Google+ local, but it is also true with Google+ (non-Local) business pages and Google+ personal profiles.

GET

GOOGLE+!

Google+ is actually not one but two and a half different social networks:

Google+ Business Pages. These are the business pages on Google+, the Fords, Toyotas, and Whole Foods corporate accounts by which businesses promote their wares and connect with customers.

Google+ Local Pages. Now called "Google My Business," these are business pages, similar to those on Yelp, that focus on local search.

Reviews on Google. Google has split off reviews from Google+, creating a strange situation in which reviews "live" on Google+ even though company pages "live" on Google+.

And finally there's the Google +1 button (http://jmlinks.com/18x) (someone "votes" for your website as cool and shares it with his or her friends on Google+). With Google+nearly dead as a social network, it's not clear that this button has a huge impact on SEO, but it certainly won't hurt!

Google+ Business Pages: Not Great Value, But Easy to Set Up

We'll look at Google+ Local in detail in the next chapter, so let's start our examination of Google+ with the **Google+ Business Page** first. This is essentially the same concept as business pages on Facebook. You set up a business page, people "like" you ("circle" you), and thereby when you share messages on Google+, they will see these messages in their news feed on the Google+ social network. From an SEO perspective, being active on Google+ at a business or corporate level probably helps your SEO. It also has a big impact on your branded search terms.

Heretofore, there isn't a lot of real activity on Google+, so I don't recommend spending a lot of time on Google+ for business. In fact, let's face it. Google+ is pretty much a failure.

But until Google pulls the official plug on its embarrassingly pathetic social network, it may continue to have an impact on SEO. It's free and easy, so why not use it? Use a program like Hootsuite (http://hootsuite.com/) and you can simultaneously post to Faceobook, Google+, LinkedIn, etc., so you might as well duplicate what you post to Facebook to Google+ and you've helped your SEO, if only a little bit.

Learn more about Google+ for business at https://business.google.com/, formally called "Google My Business."

Google+ at an Individual Level

Next, let's turn to Google+ at an individual level. **Google+ Profile** pages give individuals the opportunity to position themselves as "industry experts." Setting up a Google+ profile for each of your bloggers is, therefore, a useful if minimal **todo** for successful social media SEO. One thing that Google+ does bring to the table is that if someone "follows" you on Google+, and you share content that matches one of their Google queries, then your picture and your content can show on Google for that user, if (and only if) they are signed in to their Google account. Here's a screenshot of what you'll see if you follow me on Google+, you're signed into your Google account,

What Makes a Website Trustworthy to Google? Google search quality ...
https://plus.**google**.com/104682685052057072673/posts/LS3bdfEQkBr ▾
Jason McDonald
Jul 6, 2016 - **Google** search quality guidelines. The humans have spoken as to what makes a website SEO 'trustworthy!' http://selnd.com/29r7yHm. What Makes a Website ...

In addition, Google+ / Google sends email alerts to people admonishing them to login to Google+ because they've missed such-and-such post on Google+, meaning that by participating in Google+ you get "push" emails generated for you by Google.

VIDEO. Watch a video tutorial on how to use Google+ personal to influence search results at http://jmlinks.com/17x.

In summary, set up both a corporate Google+ page and personal Google+ page(s) for key employee(s), so that Google knows you "love" Google+! The reality is that Google+

hasn't been much of a success, but it's easy to set up and it might have some positive benefit on your SEO – so why not?

≫≫ DELIVERABLE: A COMPLETED SOCIAL MEDIA SEO WORKSHEET

The **DELIVERABLE** for this chapter is a completed "Social Media SEO worksheet." For the worksheet, go to https://www.jm-seo.org/workbooks/ (enter the code 'fitness' to register if you have not already done so), and click on the link to the "Social Media SEO worksheet."

SURVEY OFFER

CLAIM YOUR $10 REBATE OR FREE BOOK! HERE'S HOW –

19. Visit http://jmlinks.com/survey.
20. Take a short, simple survey about the book.
21. Indicate whether you want a $10.00 rebate or a free copy of one of Jason's other books on SEO / Social Media Marketing / Job Search & Career-building.

WE WILL THEN –

- Rebate you the $10.00, or send you a free copy of one of the other books.

~ $10 REBATE OFFER ~

~ LIMITED TO ONE PER CUSTOMER ~

EXPIRES: 3/1/2017

SUBJECT TO CHANGE WITHOUT NOTICE

GOT QUESTIONS? CALL 800-298-4065

5.3

LOCAL SEO

Many Google searches are **local** in nature. Searches like "pizza," "divorce attorney," or even "SEO consultants" tend to have a local nature, and Google is pretty good at inferring which searches have a local character. Users in turn often append geographic terms to their Google searches such as "NYC" or "SF" to clarify to Google that they want "Watch Repair NYC" rather than "Watch Repair Online" and so forth and so on. So if you have a clearly **local** business (*a roofing company, a CPA firm, a watch repair shop, a personal injury law firm, a hypnosis practice...*), **local SEO** is a must.

Even if your business isn't entirely local, local can still be quite relevant as can reviews. Local search, as we shall see, is heavily dependent on **customer reviews**. Understanding review marketing can help any company with its SEO, not just local companies.

Let's get started!

TODO LIST:

» Understand Local Search Opportunities

» Claim and Optimize Your Local Social Media

» Cross-link Your Website to Your Local Social Media

» Understand & Accept the Review Revolution

» Create a Review Marketing Strategy

» How to Help Your Customers Write Reviews

» Identify Reputation Management & Review Opportunities

»» Deliverable: A Local SEO Worksheet

» UNDERSTAND LOCAL SEARCH OPPORTUNITIES

Local search is huge on the Internet. People search for "Dallas Roofer" or "Hypnotherapist New York City" or even just "Sushi." Conduct an inventory of your search keywords and note which queries produce prominent Google Local results. Searches for **single** or **short tail** keywords such as "Sushi" or "Divorce Attorney" often produce localized results; take note of which single or short tail searches are especially relevant.

For example, here's a screenshot of the search for "Sushi":

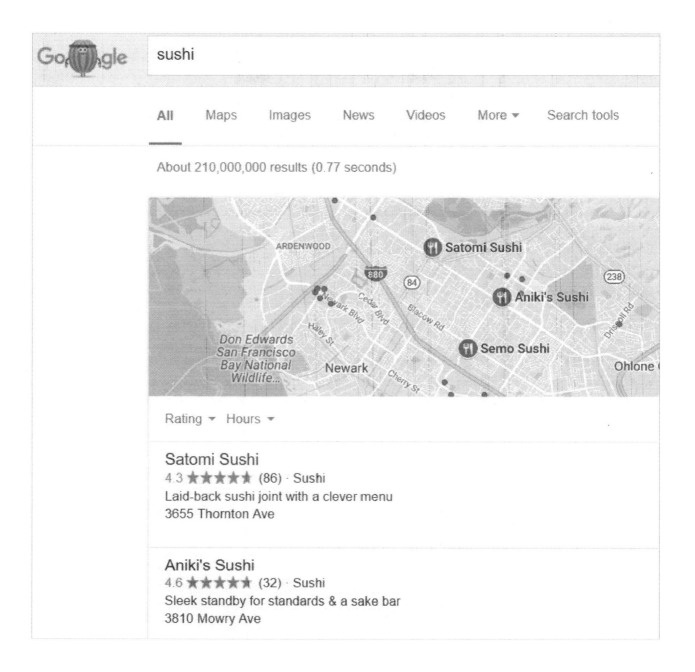

The three results that appear with stars are called the "snack pack" and are driven by Google+ / Google reviews. Secondly, even searches that you would not think might be localized such as "SEO Consultant" may in fact be localized. For example, "SEO Consultant" yields different localized results in Fremont, California, and in Tulsa, Oklahoma. You can use the Google Ad Preview tool at http://jmlinks.com/14y to change your location and view results "as if" you were in different cities.

VIDEO. Watch a video tutorial on how to switch your city location and view localized Google results at http://jmlinks.com/17s.

Your first **TODO** is to look at the keywords from your keyword worksheet, and test them to see if a) they show the local "snack pack" results, and/or b) if results vary by location. If so, then localized SEO is very important to your success. If not, local doesn't matter so much, but reviews may still be important (*see below*).

(*Google Local has now been ignominiously renamed "Google My Business," but I will refer to it as Google Local to avoid the nasty tongue-twister of 'Optimize your company's "Google My Business" page*).

Second, keep an eye out for other services like Yelp, YP.com, or Citysearch popping up prominently in your local search results. Here's a search for "Watch Repair NYC," for example:

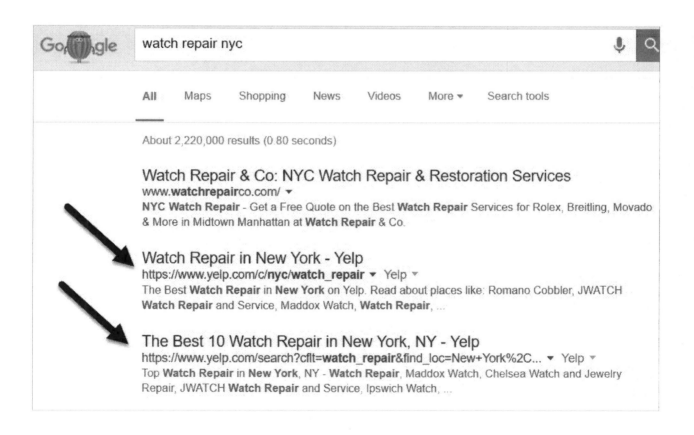

Notice how the #2 and #3 results are for Yelp.com. Your customers may not realize that first they do a Google search, and then they end up on Yelp. They may indicate they "found you on the Internet" or "found you on Google" when in fact they jumped from Google to a local search engine such as Yelp or YP.com.

As for Bing, note that Yelp has a very significant impact on Bing results (as Bing lacks its own local review system). Here's a screenshot of "sushi" on Bing:

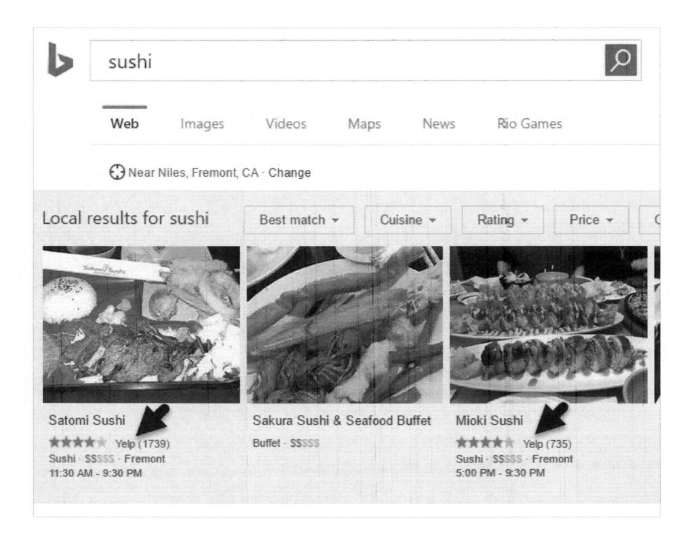

Again, consumers may think that they came from Bing or the Internet, when in fact they came first from Bing and then to Yelp and then to your company.

Google Local Keeps Changing

With Google+ in complete disarray, Google continues to make erratic changes to the format of its local results, on both the desktop and on the phone. Currently, the common format is what's called the "Snackpack," three top results in the local listings usually indicated by stars. A few things of note here:

- The more reviews a company has, the more likely it is to appear at the top of the three free local listings.
- Review stars are driven by reviews exclusively on Google, despite the fact that few consumers actually use Google / Google+ to write reviews.
- On the phone, AdWords ads often dramatically crowd down the "free" local listings as well as the "organic" listings.
- The local SEO-optimized listings appear below the "snack pack."

Consumer may ignore both the ads and the local Google+ listings and proceed to the organic results below them. Or they may be confused as to what is a local result, what's an organic result, and what is an ad.

If local search matters to your company, the take-aways here, are:

- Many searches produce the Google+ local "Snackpack," usually consisting of the top three local results.
- Reviews have a huge impact on who shows in the top results, and these are reviews on Google, requiring a Google / Google+ account by the consumer.
- Local results can also appear underneath the "Snackpack," as well as on other types of searches that Google localizes without producing the "Snackpack."

Behind the scenes, your localized profile (such as reviews) may influence whether you show even if the "snack pack" itself isn't showing.

» CLAIM AND OPTIMIZE YOUR LOCAL SOCIAL MEDIA

Your second **TODO** is to claim your local listings. To find and claim your listing, start at Google My Business (https://business.google.com/) and follow the instructions to find and claim your listing there. Be sure to claim your listing with an email address (such as a gmail) and Google account that is a corporate asset, as it is quite difficult to transfer a Google+ Local listing from one user to another!

VIDEO. Watch a video on how to find your business on Google+ local at http://jmlinks.com/17d.

Important: safeguard the email address and password by which you claimed your listing as it is very, very difficult to reset a Google+ local password!

Optimizing Your Business Listing on Google

To be honest, Google has made a complete mess of Google local. It's very frustrating for small business owners, so be patient and just accept the train wreck of complexity that is Google local. (I personally wish they'd focus a bit less on self-driving cars and a bit more on a better small business marketing experience, but they haven't called me for advice!). Here are the steps:

- Find and claim your business at Google My Business (https://business.google.com/). You may need to request, receive, and verify via postcard. I recommend setting up a specific gmail email address for this purpose.
- Click on your business, and click on the red "edit" button to edit your business name, website, location, hours, etc.
- Add photos of your business by clicking on "Manage photos." (Note: these photos will often appear when someone Googles the name of your business in a branded or reputational search, with no indication of where they came from).
- Update your business description to include your target keywords in a nice, succinct summary and link FROM your business description TO your website. To edit your business description, while staying logged in, go to https://aboutme.google.com/. On the far right, click on your name / photo, and

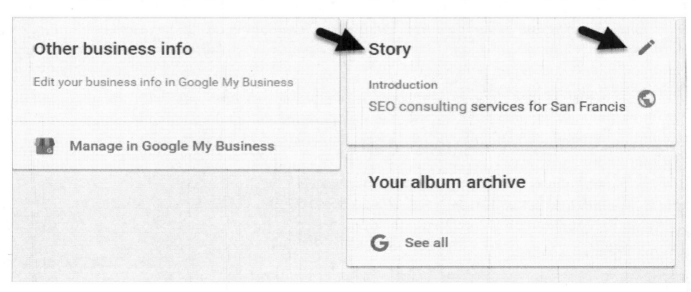

make sure you switch over to your business. Then click on the pencil to the right of "Story." Here's a screenshot:

It's not clear if optimizing your listing has a big impact, but you might as well optimize your business listing description. You can also edit your business information by Googling your business name, while being signed into the account that controls your listing.

By claiming your listing, you will also be able to respond to customer reviews.

The Steps to Google+ Local Success

Whether you are a Dallas dog groomer, a New York pizza restaurant, or a Seattle artisan coffeehouse, the steps are the same:

- **Identify** and **claim** your Google+ listing for your local business.
- **Optimize** the listing description and categories with keyword-heavy content as well as links back to your website.
- Begin **posting** to Google+, especially on keyword-relevant topics. (See Chapter 5.2 on Social Media for more information, and use Hootsuite (http://hootsuite.com/) to manage your Google+ posting strategy).
- Get **followers** and **views**.
- Solicit **reviews** from happy customers (more about this below).

Beyond Google+, **find**, **claim**, and **optimize** your other local listings across the major sites. Here's a list of the most important sites for social media at a local level:

Yelp (http://biz.yelp.com/) (No. 2 in importance after Google!)

Others (all about the same in importance) –

Citysearch (http://www.citysearch.com/)
Bing Places (https://www.bingplaces.com/)
CitySearch (http://www.insiderpages.com/)

Yelp is #2 after Google for Local SEO Impact

After Google+ Local, Yelp is No. 2. It has a huge impact on Bing search results, and Yelp often appears high on Google organic search results pages, driving consumers FROM Google TO Yelp. Claim your listing at http://biz.yelp.com/ and be sure to optimize your business description by writing keyword-heavy text about your business on Yelp.

> **VIDEO.** Watch video tutorials on how to claim and optimize your Yelp listing, at http://jmlinks.com/16x and http://jmlinks.com/16w.

After Google+ and Yelp, claim and optimize your 2nd tier listings such as Citysearch or YellowPages. A couple nifty services that help you identify and claim your local listings are at https://moz.com/local and http://www.yext.com/. For free, they'll scan what's out there; for a fee they will help you optimize the second-tier listing services after Google+ and Yelp.

> **VIDEO.** Watch a video tutorial on how to use Yext and MOZ to claim your second-tier local listings at http://jmlinks.com/18c.

» CROSS-LINK YOUR WEBSITE TO YOUR LOCAL SOCIAL MEDIA

Once you've successfully claimed your listings, it's time to cross-link your website to your listings, especially Google+ and Yelp. Your third **TODO** is to cross-link the website to the listing URLs. Your listing on Google+, Yelp, and other local review sites should have a) the **same** address and **telephone number** as on your website, and b) a **link** to your website. This is called a **NAP** (Name / Address / Phone) **citation**, and you want citations to be consistent across the Web. It is very, very important to use the same address and same phone number consistently across all the local listing sites as well as your own website. Please do this accurately!

Next, do this in reverse: link FROM your website TO your local listings, especially on Google and Yelp.

Preferably on your home page, or at least on your "about" or "contact us" pages, add a link from your website to the direct listing on Google and Yelp. The local listing URLS can be quite long and you must get them exactly correct. Be sure that your physical address and local phone number appears on your website!

By using a consistent name, address, and phone number across your listings and by cross-referencing them to each other, you help Google "see" which website goes with which listings. Make it easy for Google to localize your website, and Google will reward you with better rankings. The same is true for Bing and Yahoo.

» UNDERSTAND & ACCEPT THE REVIEW REVOLUTION

Reviews have changed the way that customers perceive companies, products, and services. Consider, for a moment, how you use Amazon.com as a good example. Most of us do a quick search on Amazon for a product we're interested in, scroll down and read the reviews, and if the reviews are positive (and the price is right) are very inclined to buy the product. If the reviews are bad or scathing, then we are very unlikely to buy the product.

The same goes for finding a local sushi restaurant on Yelp, a local painter on Google, and a great place to rent a summer cottage at Lake Tahoe on VRBO.com. Even when people are looking for a place to work, reviews on sites like Glass Door (https://www.glassdoor.com/) matter a great deal.

Reviews have revolutionized how customers perceive companies, products, and services. It's a huge revolution, creating enormous opportunities for smart companies and enormous pitfalls for companies who do not know how to survive and prosper in this new environment.

The Review Dilemma

Reviews cross SEO into social media. Here's the problem. Outside of "fun" activities like going out to eat, getting coffee, going to Disneyland, or seeing local community theater, there's a big, big problem with reviews on the Internet:

- the **MOST LIKELY** person to write a review of your local business is the **UNHAPPY** customer;
- therefore, if you do nothing, you are **LIKELY** to get only **NEGATIVE REVIEWS**; but
- the **OFFICIAL** policy of Google+, Yelp, and other services is "**THOU SHALT NOT SOLICIT REVIEWS**."

Now if you are a restaurant, coffee house, or some other "fun" type of business, this may not be a big problem. People will spontaneously write reviews of restaurants and other fun businesses. In that case, you may just need to pro-actively ask happy customers, "Hey, could you do me a favor? Go on Google+ (or Yelp) and write an honest review of your experience. We'd really appreciate it!."

Video. Watch a video tutorial on how to generate easy URLs to ask customers for reviews at http://jmlinks.com/18b.

Despite what Google and Yelp say, aside from restaurants, bars, and other fun types of businesses, getting reviews is very problematic for your average small business. The most likely person to write a review is the "unhappy camper," which dramatically tilts reviews in a negative direction.

Let's take an example: a plumber. Here's the scenario:

My toilet overflows. I panic. I call a plumber, after finding him on Google (Google+), and noting he has many positive reviews. He comes out, fixes my toilet, and hands me a bill. He did a good job. I'm relieved as my toilet is fixed! However, I am not overjoyed nor proud (as I would be of getting a table at an exclusive Italian restaurant in San Francisco), so I am UNLIKELY to login to Google+ or Yelp and write a positive review. I am not that excited about my toilet repair!

But let's say he doesn't do a good job. Or he overcharges. Or he's grumpy. Or the toilet breaks the next day, and he doesn't come out for free to fix it. I am now mad as hell. I think to myself, "Oh, I'll show you: I am going to go write a bad review about you on Google+, Yelp, etc.).

The point, in sum, is that the UNHAPPY customer is much, much more likely to write a review of a plumber than a HAPPY customer.

Here's a screenshot of an example bad review on Yelp:

 8/18/2015

Called this company, as it is one of the four that is under contract with OLD REPUBLIC HOME WARRANTY!!!!!!! Lady answered phone and BEFORE she would even talk to me she DEMANDED that I tell her whether or not I was using a home warranty program. Stated that it would be two days before they would send out a tech to look at water heater that was not working! I was told that they only have 5 tech's working a very large service area. POOR reviews to match poor service including CRAP customer service from OLD REPUBLIC HOME WARRANTY!!!!

The problem is worse, however, because the official policy of ALL the review systems such as Google, Yelp, CitySearch, Tripadvisor, etc. is "thou shalt not ask for reviews." Not just thou shalt not incentivize reviews: thou shalt not EVEN ask! So, outside of "fun" activities like restaurants, bars, and amusement parks, if you do nothing, you are most likely to get very few reviews, or even worse mainly negative reviews.

Let me repeat that:

If you do nothing, you are most likely to get zero, or negative reviews.

And if you do something, you are in violation of the formal terms of service. "Damned if you do," and "Damned if you don't."

Did I mention that life was fair? Because if you thought I had indicated life was fair, you weren't paying attention. It's not fair. It's not rational. And the big companies like Google or Yelp couldn't care less about you "little people" down on the ground.

You're on your own, baby.

Let's review what we've learned about reviews:

#1 Customer reviews matter!

The more reviews you have from people in your local community, people who use your target keywords in their reviews, and people who are active reviewers, the more Google will propel your website to the top of its local search results. Reviews are, in fact, a lot like links and Google clearly rewards websites that have more reviews.

REVIEWS, LIKE LINKS,

PUSH YOU TO THE TOP OF GOOGLE

#2 If you do nothing...

If you do nothing, outside of "fun" industries like restaurants or theme parks, you are likely to get zero reviews or negative reviews, while your competitors may be pro-actively soliciting reviews and ranking higher than you on Google (as well as Bing, Yelp, etc.) and getting more business.

#3 The Terms of Service

The terms of service forbid you from soliciting reviews.

#4 You Have to Pro-actively Solicit Reviews to Succeed

You have to pro-actively solicit reviews to succeed yet do so in such a way that you minimize your risk of getting in trouble.

After claiming and optimizing your local listings, your next **TODO** is to create a review solicitation process. *Encourage* your happy customers to review your business in every way possible - on Google, on Yelp, on Citysearch, and on any other local listing site important to you.

Being Pro-active about Getting Reviews

What's the solution? You must pro-actively ask HAPPY customers for reviews. Something as simple, as "are you satisfied with the plumbing job? You are... Could you do us a favor: write us a review on Google+, Yelp, etc.") – will often make a huge difference. Secondly, you might reward not the customer but rather your employee. Offer each plumber a $50.00 bonus if/when a review is posted about him and his service. In that way, the employee has an incentive to proactively ask. A service that automates the review-seeking process is **ReviewBuzz** at http://www.reviewbuzz.com/. Third, just educating everyone in the company how valuable reviews are will help employees be "on the look out" for a happy customer willing to write a positive review.

For review marketing, here's a good strategy:

- Make sure that at the **end of a successful sale**, your customer is politely asked to review you on Google Places, Yelp, Google Merchant Center (Google Shopping), etc. Make "Please review us!" part of your sales process.
- Think of using **real-world promotions** to encourage reviews such as stickers, cards, brochures at your place of business that ask people to "find you" on social media sites like Google or Yelp. Make sure your customer relations staff is primed to understand how important reviews are, and mention it to happy customers.
- Use **follow up emails** with customers as well as social media like Facebook to thank people who have already reviewed you, and to encourage people who might.

I am NOT advocating paying for reviews, and I am NOT advocating faking reviews. However, a polite "could you do us a favor?" will go a long way towards increasing your review count. When you have a happy customer willing to write a review, it is worth doing everything in your power up to and including helping them with the technical details to get them to write a review for you, especially on Google.

Remember that, technically speaking, it is a *violation* of terms of service to solicit paid reviews, so encourage reviews in a judicious and polite manner! Paying for reviews can be dangerous because, if discovered, your site may be removed from Google, Yelp, or another service.

Legal Disclaimer

You are responsible for everything you do in terms of your Internet marketing. Nothing I am writing here should be construed as required or recommended advice. Legally, I am recommending that you do nothing in terms of review solicitation. I am merely pointing out how many companies "solicit reviews."

Take responsibility for your own actions as a marketer, and act on your own risk!

More sophisticated strategies are discussed in my *Social Media Marketing Workbook* in the chapter on "Yelp Local," available on Amazon at http://jmlinks.com/smm.

Encouraging **positive** reviews in a judicious manner is a critical part of local SEO, despite official policies of Google+, Yelp, and other review sites.

» HOW TO HELP YOUR CUSTOMERS WRITE REVIEWS

We'll assume you've found, claimed, and optimized your Google listing as well as your Yelp listing. If you're in a specific industry such as vacation rentals, we'll assume you've identified sites like Tripadvisor, AirBnB, or VRBO, and found, claimed, and optimized those listings as well. We'll assume you have a "happy camper" who is willing to write you an honest review about their experience. They might find it technically daunting however. So how do you help them with the technical details?

- Find your Google listing using the Grade.us review link generator at http://jmlinks.com/14z or simply go to Google, Google your company, and click on the blue link to your reviews.
- Copy the huge URL that is generated by Google.
- Go to a URL shortening service such as Bitly.com or TinyURL.com and "shorten" that huge URL into something easy like http://tinyurl.com/reviewjasonsf (If you click on that, you'll see it in action).

Similarly, for Yelp, go to http://www.yelp.com/, find your company on Yelp, copy your URL, and shorten it.

Next, write a sample email that you can send out to a happy customer after the sale, such as:

> Greetings!
>
> Thank you so much for the opportunity to be your Tulsa roofing company. We really appreciate the business, and if you have any questions or issues, please do not hesitate to reach us immediately. Your satisfaction is our #1 concern.
>
> If you have a moment, we would really appreciate a short, honest review on one of the major local services. Here's how:
>
> Google
>
> Go to http://tinyurl.com/review-our-company
>
> Click on the blue "write a review" button
>
> You may need to login to your Google / Google+ account.
>
> Thank you in advance,
>
> Bob Jones
>
> Your Local Roofer

VIDEO. Watch a video tutorial on how to generate easy URLs to ask customers for reviews at http://jmlinks.com/18b.

Again, technically speaking this is a violation of terms of service. Yelp, in particular, is quite nasty about policing its review system. However, you are NOT paying for a review, and you are NOT getting a faked review. So, with you assuming 100% liability, this is one strategy to increase your review count.

Pre-Screen Customers to Find the Happy Campers

In addition, I recommend that you pre-screen customers, asking ONLY those who are happy for a review. If they are unhappy, either a) fix the problem (and then ask for a review) or, b) do NOT ask them for a review. ReviewBuzz (http://www.reviewbuzz.com/) and ReputationStacker (https://reputationstacker.com) use this tactic. However, whether this will come under fire by Yelp and Google, remains to be seen.

≫ RESPONDING TO REVIEWS

Should you respond to reviews? First and foremost, I recommend that you create a pro-active policy to nurture positive reviews about your company, product, or service. If the only reviews you still get are negative, then you have a much bigger problem than your SEO and SMM! Second, you do not need to respond to positive reviews, but you can if you like. It doesn't really matter. Third, if / when you receive a negative review, try to fix the problem for the customer. However, if the customer is a total jerk, that may not be possible. In that case:

- **Calm down**. DO NOT WRITE BACK IN ANGER or TALK TRASH back.
- **Wait a week** or so and see if the review is filtered out. Especially on Yelp, many reviews get filtered out.
- If not, **compose a dignified, respectful response** that states your side of the issue.
- **Realize that you are NOT talking to the angry reviewer**. Rather you are talking to other customers who will be reading this interchange.

Indeed, I do NOT recommend responding to a negative review, especially on Yelp, at first. Yelp's filter may block them out, but if you respond, you are indicating to Yelp that this is, indeed, a real customer. Your best strategy is to "swamp" negative reviews with positive reviews by real customers, again with the caveat that unless you pro-actively encourage happy customers (outside of "fun" industries) you will receive few reviews or only negative reviews.

>> IDENTIFY REPUTATION MANAGEMENT AND REVIEW OPPORTUNITIES

Review marketing doesn't apply only in terms of local SEO, however. Be sure to pay attention to your **branded** and **reputational** searches. Examples are:

> *Company name – branded search: Geico, Bank of America*
>
> *Company name plus terms like reviews – reputational search such as "Geico Reviews" or "Reviews of Bank of America."*

Google your branded and reputational searches on a regular basis, and watch out for negative attacks against your company. The best defense against nasty negative press online is to pro-actively optimize the Web with positive brand mentions about your company.

Claim and Optimize Your Social Profiles

Your best step is to claim and SEO-optimize your relevant social media sites (e.g., Facebook, Twitter, LinkedIn, etc.), as well as create a few duplicate websites, if necessary, optimized on your company name and helper words such as *reviews*. In addition, generate press releases and syndicate them via a service like CISION, with your company name and branded terms. Build links to these social media listings and websites.

Be sure to label your "testimonials" page, "reviews." This will often be the #1 result for a Google search such as "Your company name reviews."

The point here is to use SEO to prophylactically prevent unhappy customers from attacking your brand online. (*Now, of course, do everything you can to have truly happy customers and prevent the "customer from Hell" from arising in the first place*).

Your **TODOS** in terms of **reputation management** SEO are:

- **Identify your branded terms** (company name) plus your reputational phrases (usually company name plus terms like reviews).
- **Monitor these searches** on Google and Bing.

- Prophylactically, **set up and SEO-optimize your major social profiles** such as Facebook, Twitter, LinkedIn, etc. (even if they have zero social value – you are doing this for the SEO value in terms of reputation management) including the "about" or "reviews" (testimonials) page on your website.
- Use **press releases** and **micro websites** to crowd out the top results on Google for your company name and/or reputational searches.

To see this in action, Google "JM Internet Group Reviews" (http://jmlinks.com/7v). Notice how Google is full of all of the social media sites as well as press releases for the company. Now, obviously, we have only happy customers! But the point is that we have SEO-optimized for our branded term and reputational term in advance of any negative attack by an unhappy customer or competitor. Reputation management, in short, is an important task for effective search engine optimization on your branded and reputational terms.

▶▶ DELIVERABLE: A LOCAL SEO WORKSHEET

The **DELIVERABLE** for this chapter is a completed "Local SEO Worksheet. For the worksheet, go to https://www.jm-seo.org/workbooks (click on "SEO Fitness 2017," and enter the code '2017fitness' to register if you have not already done so), and click on the link to the "Local SEO Worksheet."

6.1
METRICS

Google Analytics is the best free Web metrics tool available today. It is, however, only a tool: it doesn't tell you what to measure, nor what to do with the information you acquire. Before you even start with Analytics, your first step is to think through *what* you want to measure, and *why* you want to measure it. Common metrics are your *rank* on Google for target keyword queries, *traffic sources* or how people find your website, your top *landing pages*, your *bounce rate*, and whether landings on your website convert into *goals*, such as registrations or sales. Second, after you've identified what you want to measure, you need to turn to not just Google Analytics but other metrics tools and understand how to use them. They're not easy to use! Third, there are even more advanced techniques that can "slice and dice" your data so that you truly know what's going on with your website. Finally, there's no point in getting all this data unless you do something with it, so you need to take the knowledge gained from Analytics and turn it into actionable todos.

Let's get started!

TODO LIST:

>> Define What to Measure

>> Measure Your SERP Rank, Domain Authority, & Social Metrics

>> Use Google Search Console (Webmaster Tools)

>> Use Google Analytics Basic Features

>> Use Advanced Features in Google Analytics

>> >> Deliverable: Google Analytics Worksheet

>> Deploy Circular Analytics for Improved SEO

Metrics, especially as seen through the prism of Google Analytics, can seem overwhelming. Most marketers and small business owners want to measure whether they are ranking on Google, whether they're getting traffic, and whether that traffic is converting (or not) into sales or sales leads as indicated by feedback forms. In terms of more specific items, here is a breakdown of things you should commonly measure or record every month on the 1st of the month:

1. **Your Rank on Google Searches.** SEO starts with whether your website is in position 1, 2, or 3 on Google or at least page one. Using your keywords as identified on your keyword worksheet, you want to measure your rank on Google and its improvement over time. By knowing which keywords you rank well for, and which you rank poorly for, you'll know where you need to concentrate your efforts.

2. **Your Domain Authority and Links.** Off Page SEO is all about links, so you want to use a tool like MOZ.com or AHREFS.com and measure the domain authority of your website, and the number of inbound links. With your link-building efforts, this should improve over time.

3. **Social Media & Reviews.** Social media is increasingly important for Off Page SEO, so you want to measure your "followers" on Twitter, your "likes" on Facebook, and your "followers" on LinkedIn for your company page. In addition, if local matters to you, you want to keep track of your **review count** on Google and Yelp. Through your promotion efforts, you want to see an increase in **followers** and **reviews** over time.

4. **Traffic Sources.** Turning to Google Search Console and Google Analytics, you want to measure your "traffic sources" to learn how people *find* your website, especially your best performing keywords and referrer websites.

5. **User Behavior.** Once they land on your website, do they convert to a sale or sales lead, or do they just browse around and leave? Learn what people *do* once they land on your website, especially marketing goals such as registrations or completed sales. Understand *successes* and *failures* and investigate ways to improve your conversion rate.

For your first **TODO**, call a marketing meeting, sit down with a blank piece of paper or a Word / Google doc, and brainstorm what metrics are most important to you as a marketer. How do people find you? What do they do once they land on your website? What background metrics, such as rank on Google and reviews on Google or Yelp, turbocharge your success on Google? Identify these and other questions that can be translated into something concrete to measure.

≫ Measure Your SERP Rank, PageRank, & Social Metrics

Your **SERP rank** (Search Engine Results Page) measures your website's position on a target search query. Your **PageRank** or **Domain Authority**, in contrast, is a measurement of your authority on the Web. It is not really publicly released, so use third-party tools such as MOZ.com or AHREFS.com that will give you your **domain authority**. As we learned in link building, think of your **Web Authority** as a measurement of how important your site is on the Web.

Measure Your Rank on Google for Target Keywords

To measure your SERP rank, the best free tool is Rank Checker by SEOBook (http://www.seobook.com/). The tool is available only on Firefox. After installing it, go to Tools > Rank Checker > Options and set the "delay between queries" to 99 seconds. This is because if you run a long keyword list, Google will stop providing rank data to the tool. Then to run the tool from Firefox, go to Tools >Rank Checker > Run > Add Multiple Keywords. Enter your domain and keyword list, hit start and the tool will measure your rank on Google and Bing.

> **Video.** Watch a video tutorial of how to use the Rank Checker tool at http://jmlinks.com/18y.

MOZ.com, AHREFS.com, SERPS.com, and other vendors have paid tools that can easily automate your rank checking efforts. These are easier to use, and cost around $99 / month.

Check Your Localized Rank for Short Tail Searches

RankChecker does not measure your localized rank in the "Snackpack" or first three local results. To measure this, city-by-city, you need to manually change cities and enter your keywords. You can do this inside of AdWords by clicking on Tools > Ad Preview and Diagnosis. If you do not have an AdWords account, you can access this tool at http://jmlinks.com/15g or on my dashboard at http://jmlinks.com/seodash and then the local section.

> **VIDEO.** Watch a video tutorial on how to check local rank at http://jmlinks.com/17s.

Record Your Rank Each Month

Your second **TODO** is to revisit your **keyword worksheet** and input your rank for target sample phrases, including your rank for local cities if applicable. I usually create a tab called "sample keywords" and measure my rank on Google keyword queries before I start an SEO project, after I have implemented the "on page" changes, and every month thereafter. I then look for ranks *greater than ten* as bad, *greater than three* as in trouble and work on those priority keywords.

Domain & Link Metrics

Secondarily, I recommend you measure your **domain authority** as a surrogate for Google PageRank on a monthly basis. Go to Open Site Explorer at http://jmlinks.com/7y, input your website home page URL, and note the three metrics at the top of the page: domain authority, root domains, and spam score. Record each of these on your keyword worksheet each month. Here's a screenshot for jm-seo.org:

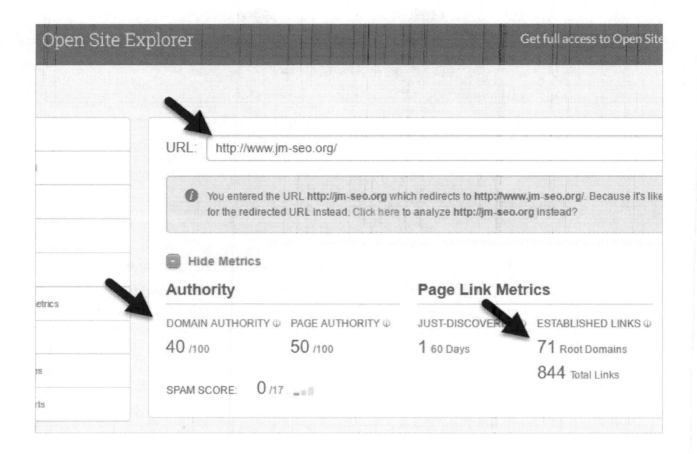

Domain authority is a surrogate for Google PageRank, or a metric that measures how important Google thinks your website is. A site like *nytimes.com* might be 100, whereas *jm-seo.org* is a 40, and a tiny, unimportant site might be a 7. What's important is your domain authority relative to competitors, and whether this improves over time. **Root domains** is the number of websites that link to you: again, you want this to grow over time. You can see here it's a 71, meaning 71 websites link to the domain. The **Spam score** is an attempt, after Google's Penguin update, to measure whether your site is on the "naughty list" or not.

Another good site to use for this purpose is AHREFS.com. In any case, you want to measure on a monthly basis your link footprint.

Social Media Metrics

Third, measure your followers on Google+ and Twitter, your page views, and your review count on Yelp and Google+. You want these all to move in a positive direction, over time. Increasingly, SEO is "going social," so it's a good time to be aware of how your social authority is improving over time.

If you are a local business, **reviews** are incredibly important. So on your keyword worksheet, create a tab called "social" and add in your social media sites such as Google or Yelp that have customer reviews. Chart the number and the average star score each month.

» Use Google Search Console (Webmaster Tools)

We'll assume you've claimed your **Google Search Console** (Webmaster Tools) account as well as the corresponding **Webmaster Tools** account on Bing. These give you some unique items that are not available in Google Analytics. First and foremost, Google Search Console will give you a rough idea of your **inbound keyword queries**. On the left hand menu, click Search Traffic > Search Analytics. Next, check all the boxes (clicks, impressions, CTR, and position). Now you'll have a list of keywords that people are searching for by impressions, and the number of clicks to your website. You can sort the data by impressions, clicks, etc. Take this data with a grain of salt, as it's not clear that it's entirely accurate but it gives you some data on the keywords people are entering, for which you rank on Google, and the clicks from Google to your website.

Next, in the same section, click on **Links to Your Site**. Then click on the MORE button on the bottom under "who links the most." Then click on "download latest links." Here's a screenshot:

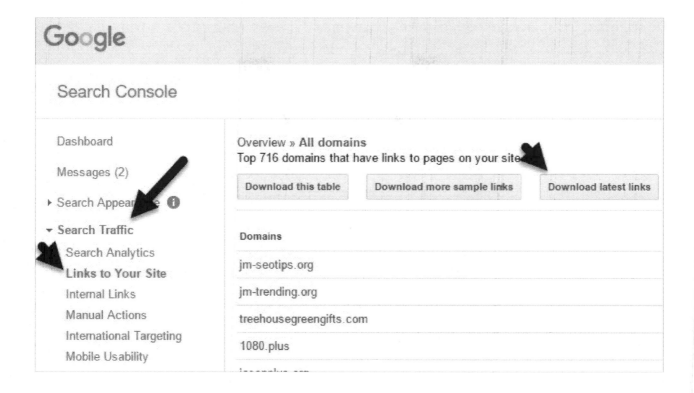

Here, you can view and download links to your site as discovered by Google. With an active link-building effort, you should see an improvement over time and you can monitor the exact, new sites that are linking to you.

Finally, I like to take a quick peek at Google Index > Content Keywords and verify that the words there are, generally speaking, my keyword targets.

You can link Google Search Console into Google Analytics, so you can see this data in one place. For information on how to link them, visit http://jmlinks.com/15b.

As for Bing Webmaster Tools, similar data is available.

> **VIDEO.** Watch a video tutorial on how to use Google Webmaster Tools (Search Console) at http://jmlinks.com/17u.

>> USE GOOGLE ANALYTICS BASIC FEATURES

Now that you have these measurements, it's time to dive into Google Analytics (https://www.google.com/analytics). If you haven't already, install the required tracking code on all pages of your website. If you're using WordPress you can use the MonsterInsights WordPress plugin for Google Analytics at http://jmlinks.com/8e.

Alternatively, the latest and greatest way to install Google Analytics is to install Google Tag Manager (https://tagmanager.google.com/) and then follow the instructions to install Google Analytics "on top of" tag manager. Learn more at http://jmlinks.com/15c.

Once you have installed the Javascript code on your site and allowed enough time to elapse for data to accumulate, it's time for some basic Analytics. Log in to Analytics, and scroll down the left hand menu. Here's a run-down:

- Click on **Audience**, to see basic data about how many visitors are coming to your website daily, where they are coming from, and basic traffic sources such as search engines vs. referring sites.
  - Click on **Geo** to see where your website visitors come from by country, state, and even city.
  - Click on **Technology** to see browsers that they use (e.g., Chrome, Firefox, Edge, Safari).
  - Click on **Mobile** to see your web traffic: desktop vs. tablet vs. phones, and even phone types.
  - Click on **User Flow** for a nice, pictorial map of how people "flow" through your website.
- Click on **Acquisition** and browse "referring" sites such as blogs, portals, news releases, etc., that are sending users from their website to yours via clicks.
  - Click on **Channels** to see how people get to your website, by *direct* (URLs and bookmarks), *organic search* (Search Engines), *referral* (links from other sites) and *social* (social media sites like Facebook or Twitter).
  - Click on **Source / Medium** and **Referrals** for another view of the above data.
  - Click on **AdWords** if you are running advertisements on Google; here, you can get data down to the keyword level.
  - Click on **Search Console, Queries** to see which keywords and key phrases are performing well for you in generating incoming web traffic. (Link your Google Analytics to your Google Webmaster Tools or Search Console for this feature).
  - Click on **Social** for detail on social media networks; click on Users Flow here for a pictorial representation.
  - Click on **Campaigns** to see activity you have "tagged" as a campaign or UTM string. (To "tag" inbound links as from a Bing advertising campaign, a Facebook or Twitter campaign, etc., see http://jmlinks.com/15d.)
- Click on **Behavior** to see what people do on your website.

- o Click on **Behavior Flow** for a nice, pictorial map of how people "flow" through your website.
- o Click on **Site Content** and then drill down to **All Pages** (your most trafficked pages), **Landing Pages** (first page they touch), and **Exit Pages** (last page they touch).
- o Click on **Site Speed** for information on how fast your website is, including **Speed Suggestions**.
- o Click on **In-Page Analytics** for a nifty way to browse your website page by page and get information on what elements people click on in percentage terms. **Note**: install the Page Analytics Plugin for Chrome (http://jmlinks.com/18z) for an amazing view on how people click around your website.

- • Click on **Conversions** to see whether traffic is "converting," usually buying stuff on eCommerce and/or filling out feedback forms as sales leads.
  - o Click on **Goals** (if you have defined goals, see below) to see what goals exist and whether they are converting.
  - o Click on **Overview, Reverse Goal Path,** and **Funnel Visualization** (if you have defined these elements to see the paths taken to/from a goal).
  - o
  - o Click on **eCommerce** (if you are running an eCommerce site) for information on purchases.

VIDEO. Watch a video tutorial on basic Google Analytics at http://jmlinks.com/17y.

Basic Google Analytics provides you a lot of key information on incoming web traffic such as geographic location, mobile platform, and browser version. Finally, you can click on the date field at the top far right of Analytics to change the date filter for data or to compare two time periods.

⏩ USE ADVANCED FEATURES IN GOOGLE ANALYTICS

Beyond Basic Analytics, there are advanced features in Google Analytics that you do not want to miss. First, click on **Segments** to "slice" and "dice" your data based on criteria such as "new visitors" vs. "repeat visitors" or the geographic locations from which visitors come. Google hides this feature behind the "Add Segment" area when you first login. Simply click on that to bring forth Advanced Segments:

Segments

Segments offers "pre-built segments," available on the right hand side under "System." Here you'll find segments such as "Mobile and Tablet Traffic." Click this to "filter" your data to see ONLY people coming from mobile phones and tablets, for example. Others of note are:

> **Organic Traffic**. Click here to filter and see ONLY traffic from search engines.
>
> **Paid Traffic**. Click here to filter and see ONLY traffic from AdWords and other forms of paid advertising as on Bing or Yahoo.
>
> **Referral Traffic**. Click here to filter and see ONLY traffic from links on other websites.
>
> **Sessions with Conversions**. Click here to filter and see ONLY traffic that actually converted (completed a goal or made a purchase).
>
> **Tablet and Desktop Traffic**. Click here to filter and see ONLY traffic from tablets or desktops.

The concept is to *first* click on a Segment, and *then* click the blue **Apply** button. *Next*, with these Segments on, browse other data in Google Analytics on the right menu such as the Geo information, or landing page information to see what's going on with respect to ONLY that Segment. You can enable up to four segments to compare at any given time. (For help with Google Segments, visit http://jmlinks.com/15e).

> **VIDEO.** Watch a video tutorial on Google Analytics segments at http://jmlinks.com/18a.

For example, here's a screenshot comparing "Organic Traffic" and "Referral Traffic" by looking at landing pages:

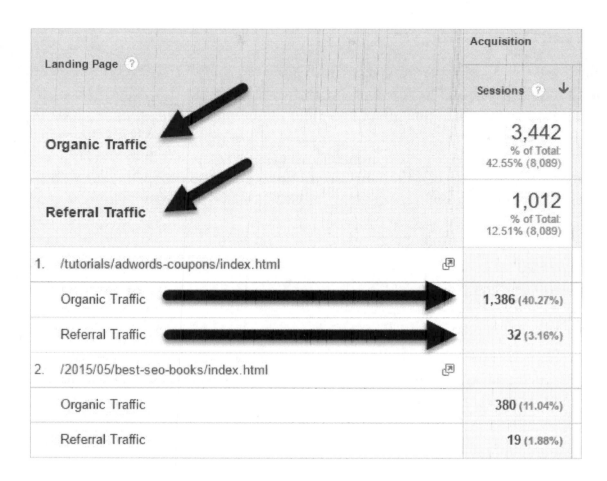

This shows that organic traffic was responsible for 1,386 visits to the AdWords Coupon page vs. only 32 for referral traffic. In this way, you can compare / contrast traffic sources or other elements as you scroll through AdWords data. It's marketing "slicing and dicing" at its best!

Custom Segments

You don't have to be content with the pre-built segments in Google Analytics. Simply click on the red "New Segment" button and follow the step-by-step wizard to create a custom segment. Scroll down the left-hand menu to filter your data by parameter; "conditions" is probably the most useful feature here. Remember to use the "Help" file (available top right, under the three dots) if you don't understand what a term means.

You can read the Google help file on how to create a custom segment at http://jmlinks.com/19b.

Goals and Conversions

Second, set up "Goals" for Analytics by registering your "Thank you" page after a registration or purchase. To do this, go to the primary log in page on Analytics by clicking on the "Admin" icon in the top right of the page. Next, click on your profile name (usually your website URL). Then click on "goals" in the middle of the page. Here is where you define a "goal" and a "funnel," which is the steps taken to reach the goal. In Advanced Analytics, you can therefore see not only how people get to your website but the steps that take as they click through your website.

> **VIDEO.** Watch a video on how to set up goals in Google Analytics at http://jmlinks.com/17z.

Once a goal is set up, you can go back to the main page in Google Analytics, and use Advanced Segments to slice and dice your data and thereby see what traffic is converting (i.e., completing your goal) vs. what is not. (For help with goals, visit the official explanation at http://jmlinks.com/19a).

Help in Google Analytics

Help is available at the top left corner under the "three dots" icon or sometimes the "gear" icon. Here's a screenshot:

"Help" is absurdly difficult to find, so if you can't find it just go to https://support.google.com/analytics/. Once there, type in your query, such as "What is a Bounce Rate?" and you'll find pretty good answers. Why Google "hides" the help feature is one of those eternal "only Google would know" questions.

Google Analytics Learning Resources

Finally, don't miss some of the free official Google videos available for learning more about Analytics. These are located at the **Google Analytics Academy** at http://jmlinks.com/8a. Ironically, these Analytics IQ Lessons are nearly impossible to find or get to from inside of Google Analytics. (They're hidden behind the graduation cap. Here's a screenshot:)

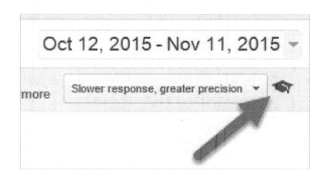

That's Google for you!

⏵⏵⏵ DELIVERABLE: GOOGLE ANALYTICS WORKSHEET

The **DELIVERABLE** for this chapter is a completed Google Analytics worksheet. For the worksheet, go to https://www.jm-seo.org/workbooks (click on "SEO Fitness 2017," and enter the code '2017fitness' to register if you have not already done so), and click on the link to the "Google Analytics worksheet."

⏵⏵ DEPLOY CIRCULAR ANALYTICS FOR IMPROVED SEO

Analytics coupled with rank measurement gives you powerful data about how you stand on Google for your target keywords, what keywords work for you in generating incoming clicks, and what people do on your website once they arrive. As with a physical fitness program, your metrics objective is to measure **before**, **during,** and **after** your SEO efforts.

Google calls this "circular analytics," whereby you measure not only how people get to your website but how they "convert" into Goals. Then you theorize new changes to your website such as new landing pages, new structural arrangements to content and text, new offers such as "free consultations" or "free events," and measure your success rate vs. your bounce rate. Your goal with circular analytics is to improve your SEO by a constant process of experimentation and measurement. In SEO, as in all things, success takes constant effort!

SURVEY OFFER

CLAIM YOUR $10 REBATE OR FREE BOOK! HERE'S HOW –

22. Visit http://jmlinks.com/survey.
23. Take a short, simple survey about the book.
24. Indicate whether you want a $10.00 rebate or a free copy of one of Jason's other books on SEO / Social Media Marketing / Job Search & Career-building.

WE WILL THEN –

- Rebate you the $10.00, or send you a free copy of one of the other books.

~ $10 REBATE OFFER ~

~ LIMITED TO ONE PER CUSTOMER ~

EXPIRES: 3/1/2017

SUBJECT TO CHANGE WITHOUT NOTICE

GOT QUESTIONS? CALL 800-298-4065

7.1

LEARNING

SEO is a competitive game that never stops evolving! The Google algorithm changes and adjusts, user behavior evolves, and your competitors also improve their SEO skills. Recently, for example, social media has become ever more important to SEO, as have both localization and personalization issues. In 2016, Google consolidated search results between mobile and desktop, and Panda and Penguin continue to evolve. New algorithm changes are no doubt in the works over at the Googleplex.

All require the successful practitioner of SEO to adapt.

"Never stop learning" must be your motto! In this Chapter, I point to resources to help you be a life-long learner.

Let's get started!

TODO LIST:

>> Download the Free Companion *SEO Toolbook*

>> Use the Worksheets

>> Bookmark and Read SEO Media Resources

>> A Final Request: Please Review me on Amazon

>> DOWNLOAD THE FREE COMPANION TOOLBOOK

The *SEO Toolbook* is a companion to this *SEO Workbook* and contains hundreds of free tools, organized by the Seven Steps. Register for **free** materials, including my SEO Toolbook, SEO Dashboard, and companion worksheets to this book at https://www.jm-seo.org/workbooks/. Click on "SEO Fitness 2017," and enter the password **2017fitness** when prompted.

You can also access my dashboard directly at http://jmlinks.com/seodash. That has links to the Toolbook, plus my favorite tools are easy to click and organized by topics / Chapters.

If you know of any other free tools, please email me as I am always on the lookout!

» USE THE WORKSHEETS, RESOURCES, VIDEOS, AND QUIZZES

Throughout this *SEO Workbook*, I have referenced helpful worksheets, videos, and resources. These follow the Seven Steps methodology and can be accessed at the book landing page after you have registered.

VIDEO. Browse available YouTube videos at http://jmlinks.com/19c.

Subscribe to my YouTube channel as well as free alerts on free toolbooks at http://jmlinks.com/free.

» BOOKMARK AND READ SEO MEDIA RESOURCES

SEO changes frequently, so I urge you to pay attention to Google directly as well as the many wonderful blogs that cover search engine optimization. Those are available in the *SEO Toolbook*.

Stay Informed: Blogs, Conferences, and Books

Among the best blogs, I recommend Danny Sullivan's Search Engine Land (http://searchengineland.com/) in particular as well as his conference called SMX (http://searchmarketingexpo.com/). I also recommend checking Amazon for new books on SEO; don't take my word for it – pay attention to what other experts and gurus say about search engine optimization. In terms of books, here's a direct link to Amazon's SEO bestseller list: http://jmlinks.com/15h. If you're looking for a "deep dive" book in terms of technical SEO, I highly recommend Eric Enge, Stephan Spencer, and Jessie Stricchiola's *The Art of SEO: Mastering Search Engine Optimization* at http://jmlinks.com/15j. It assumes you know the basics as taught in my book, and then leads you deep into the jungle of technical search engine optimization.

NEVER STOP LEARNING

If you have any problems, questions, comments, or just want to talk about life and SEO, please email me at j.mcdonald@jm-seo.net,via http://jmlinks.com/contact, or call 800-298-4065 for help. Good luck!

▶ A FINAL REQUEST: PLEASE REVIEW ME ON AMAZON

If you've read this far, I want to extend my profound thanks. It's a true labor of love to write any book, and this book has been no exception. If you have a spare moment and the spirit moves you, I would really appreciate an honest review about the *SEO Fitness Workbook* on Amazon.

- Here's a link directly to the book on Amazon: http://jmlinks.com/seo. Just visit that link and write your short, honest review of the book.

When you've done so, please send me a quick email. Thanks in advance for your support.

Never stop learning!